REVELATION

*Daily Scriptures to Receive,
Reflect, and Respond*

DR. HAROLD J. BERRY

All rights reserved. No part of this book may be reproduced, stored in a retrieval system, or transmitted in any form or by any means—electronic, mechanical, digital, photocopy, recording, or any other—except for brief quotations in printed reviews, without the prior permission of the author.

Originally published as Acts by Back to the Bible © 2020.

Copyright © 2025 by Dr. Harold J. Berry

Unless otherwise identified, all Scripture quotations in this publication are taken from the Holy Bible, New Living Translation, copyright © 1996, 2004, 2015 by Tyndale House Foundation. Used by permission of Tyndale House Publishers, Inc., Carol Stream, Illinois 60188. All rights reserved.

Cover & Interior Design: © Nelly Murariu at PixBeeDesign.com

ISBN (Paperback): 979-8-9906605-8-8

ISBN (eBook): 979-8-9906605-9-5

Dedication
Pastor Paul Pletcher

Pastor Paul and his wife, Donna, and my wife and I first became acquainted when we were living in south central Nebraska. In 2015, Paul was an interim pastor at a nearby church, and my wife, Donna, and I were in an assisted living facility for her health. My Donna went to be with Jesus in 2019.

A few of us men met for fellowship and coffee, and we asked Pastor Paul to join us. That was the beginning of our relationship that has grown and developed over the years. We communicate with each other at least once a week. We discuss theological problems, difficult Bible passages, and have good laughs when one of us tells a joke. He is closer to me than a brother, and I am honored to dedicate this volume of *Revelation: Daily Scriptures to Receive, Reflect, and Respond* to him.

Pastor Paul and his wife have been helpful to me in so many ways. One example is as I answer questions for *gotquestions.org*. Before submitting my answer, I first send it to them to see if they wish to add anything. Their many years in the ministry before retirement have given them wisdom about relationships that few people seem to possess.

Paul has been helpful in writing comments about the books I have published. In fact, the material you read on the back cover of this book was written by him.

His life is an expression of the fruit of the Spirit, mentioned in Galatians 5:22-23.

Some have said, "Every Paul needs a Timothy, and every Timothy needs a Paul." Although I am 14 years older than he is, Pastor Paul considers me his Paul, and I consider him my Timothy. Since my remarriage to a sweet and godly woman, Mary Dee, the Pletcher's and we have become close friends and prayer partners for each other.

CONTENTS

Foreword	viii

Week 1: Revelation 1
Day 1	1
Day 2	2
Day 3	3
Day 4	4
Day 5	5

Week 2: Revelation 1
Day 1	7
Day 2	8
Day 3	9
Day 4	10
Day 5	11

Week 3: Revelation 1, 2
Day 1	13
Day 2	14
Day 3	15
Day 4	16
Day 5	17

Week 4: Revelation 2
Day 1	19
Day 2	20
Day 3	21
Day 4	22
Day 5	23

Week 5: Revelation 2
Day 1	25
Day 2	26
Day 3	27
Day 4	28
Day 5	29

Week 6: Revelation 2
Day 1	31
Day 2	32
Day 3	33
Day 4	34
Day 5	35

Week 7: Revelation 2, 3
Day 1	37
Day 2	38
Day 3	39
Day 4	40
Day 5	41

Week 8: Revelation 3
Day 1	43
Day 2	44
Day 3	45
Day 4	46
Day 5	47

Week 9: Revelation 3
Day 1	49
Day 2	50
Day 3	51
Day 4	52
Day 5	53

Week 10: Revelation 4
Day 1	55
Day 2	56
Day 3	57
Day 4	58
Day 5	59

Week 11: Revelation 5
Day 1	61
Day 2	62
Day 3	63
Day 4	64
Day 5	65

Week 12: Revelation 5, 6
Day 1	67
Day 2	68
Day 3	69
Day 4	70
Day 5	71

Week 13: Revelation 6
- Day 1 … 73
- Day 2 … 74
- Day 3 … 75
- Day 4 … 76
- Day 5 … 77

Week 14: Revelation 7
- Day 1 … 79
- Day 2 … 80
- Day 3 … 81
- Day 4 … 82
- Day 5 … 83

Week 15: Revelation 7, 8
- Day 1 … 85
- Day 2 … 86
- Day 3 … 87
- Day 4 … 88
- Day 5 … 89

Week 16: Revelation 8
- Day 1 … 91
- Day 2 … 92
- Day 3 … 93
- Day 4 … 94
- Day 5 … 95

Week 17: Revelation 9
- Day 1 … 97
- Day 2 … 98
- Day 3 … 99
- Day 4 … 100
- Day 5 … 101

Week 18: Revelation 9, 10
- Day 1 … 103
- Day 2 … 104
- Day 3 … 105
- Day 4 … 106
- Day 5 … 107

Week 19: Revelation 10, 11
- Day 1 … 109
- Day 2 … 110
- Day 3 … 111
- Day 4 … 112
- Day 5 … 113

Week 20: Revelation 11
- Day 1 … 115
- Day 2 … 116
- Day 3 … 117
- Day 4 … 118
- Day 5 … 119

Week 21: Revelation 11, 12
- Day 1 … 121
- Day 2 … 122
- Day 3 … 123
- Day 4 … 124
- Day 5 … 125

Week 22: Revelation 12, 13
- Day 1 … 127
- Day 2 … 128
- Day 3 … 129
- Day 4 … 130
- Day 5 … 131

Week 23: Revelation 13
- Day 1 … 133
- Day 2 … 134
- Day 3 … 135
- Day 4 … 136
- Day 5 … 137

Week 24: Revelation 13, 14
- Day 1 … 139
- Day 2 … 140
- Day 3 … 141
- Day 4 … 142
- Day 5 … 143

Week 25: Revelation 14
- Day 1 … 145
- Day 2 … 146
- Day 3 … 147
- Day 4 … 148
- Day 5 … 149

Week 26: Revelation 14, 15
- Day 1 … 151
- Day 2 … 152
- Day 3 … 153
- Day 4 … 154
- Day 5 … 155

Week 27: Revelation 16
- Day 1 — 157
- Day 2 — 158
- Day 3 — 159
- Day 4 — 160
- Day 5 — 161

Week 28: Revelation 16
- Day 1 — 163
- Day 2 — 164
- Day 3 — 165
- Day 4 — 166
- Day 5 — 167

Week 29: Revelation 16, 17
- Day 1 — 169
- Day 2 — 170
- Day 3 — 171
- Day 4 — 172
- Day 5 — 173

Week 30: Revelation 17
- Day 1 — 175
- Day 2 — 176
- Day 3 — 177
- Day 4 — 178
- Day 5 — 179

Week 31: Revelation 17, 18
- Day 1 — 181
- Day 2 — 182
- Day 3 — 183
- Day 4 — 184
- Day 5 — 185

Week 32: Revelation 18
- Day 1 — 187
- Day 2 — 188
- Day 3 — 189
- Day 4 — 190
- Day 5 — 191

Week 33: Revelation 18, 19
- Day 1 — 193
- Day 2 — 194
- Day 3 — 195
- Day 4 — 196
- Day 5 — 197

Week 34: Revelation 19
- Day 1 — 199
- Day 2 — 200
- Day 3 — 201
- Day 4 — 202
- Day 5 — 203

Week 35: Revelation 19, 20
- Day 1 — 205
- Day 2 — 206
- Day 3 — 207
- Day 4 — 208
- Day 5 — 209

Week 36: Revelation 20
- Day 1 — 211
- Day 2 — 212
- Day 3 — 213
- Day 4 — 214
- Day 5 — 215

Week 37: Revelation 21
- Day 1 — 217
- Day 2 — 218
- Day 3 — 219
- Day 4 — 220
- Day 5 — 221

Week 38: Revelation 21
- Day 1 — 223
- Day 2 — 224
- Day 3 — 225
- Day 4 — 226
- Day 5 — 227

Week 39: Revelation 22
- Day 1 — 229
- Day 2 — 230
- Day 3 — 231
- Day 4 — 232
- Day 5 — 233

Week 40: Revelation 22
- Day 1 — 235
- Day 2 — 236
- Day 3 — 237
- Day 4 — 238
- Day 5 — 239

Personal Notes — 241

About the Author — 243

Foreword

"Enthusiastic!" That is the best word to describe my reaction after I received word that Dr Harold Berry was planning to write on the book of the Revelation. Fifty years ago, I had the pleasure of hearing Dr. Berry teach at Grace University.

From the start, Dr. Berry began impacting the University. The classroom is usually the vehicle through which professors make their impact, but Harold's teaching was never so limited.

To this day, I'm not sure if I learned more from his classes, his time in our home, or over a cup of coffee at the school's Snack Shop. I'm certain my friends would all agree. Harold Berry's "classroom" was all of our lives. We learned from him because he had, and has, integrity, devotion to God's Word, and love for those whom he taught and still teaches.

He is a main reason I followed his lead to Dallas Theological Seminary. And I continued walking his path when I later taught at Grace University for 15 years. I didn't have to start from scratch, because I had a great example as to how it was done.

Harold helped lay my theological foundation some fifty years ago, but he also taught me what discipleship, mentoring, and a loving professor looks like. I will forever be grateful for that.

Dr. Berry has extended his reach through the years with his ministry at Back to the Bible, through radio and its publications, and several books that reflect his insight and on-going mentorship to thousands. I've known many who are in ministry in a variety of ways who brighten up when his name is mentioned and who have been forever impacted by this man of God. After 43 years as a Pastor myself, I think it's possible that the greatest test this side of heaven is the impact we have on lives. My former professor passes that test with flying colors.

I'm confident his work will once again reflect careful study and scholarship, as well as a man who looks more and more like Jesus as the years go by, who is known as a friend to so many and who defines a rare combination of joy, scholarship, and passion both for God's Word and for those who study it.

Harold wears many hats: professor, author, speaker, mentor, student of God's Word, follower of Jesus, and friend. He wears them all well.

May the Lord, who alone is wise, add His wisdom, guidance, and blessing to this study.

Pastor Dan Hauge
Omaha, Nebraska

Week 1: Revelation 1

DAY 1

RECEIVE

Revelation 1:1–2

¹ This is a revelation from Jesus Christ, which God gave him to show his servants the events that must soon take place. He sent an angel to present this revelation to his servant John, ² who faithfully reported everything he saw. This is his report of the word of God and the testimony of Jesus Christ.

Notice the flow of information in these verses: It came from God the Father, to Jesus Christ, to an angel, to John. Written in Greek, the word "revelation" comes from the word *apokalupsis*, which means to "uncover" or "disclose." John was an eyewitness to what was revealed to him: the word of God and the testimony of Jesus Christ. Many prophecies in the book will be revealed.

REFLECT

Rather than thinking of it as a "Revelation of John," as the first verse indicates, it is really a "revelation of Jesus Christ" to John through an angel.

RESPOND

You need to have someone with whom you can share what you learn about the book of Revelation. It is a book that focuses on a triumphant Christ and should be encouraging to any believer in Jesus. Ask a friend to join you in this journey through the book.

Day 2

RECEIVE

Revelation 1:3

³ God blesses the one who reads the words of this prophecy to the church, and he blesses all who listen to its message and obey what it says, for the time is near.

The common remark heard about the book of Revelation is, "I can't understand it." Yet, it must be remembered that it was written by a fisherman for common people. It was not intended that only those with a graduate degree in theology would be enabled to understand the book. Plus, it promises a blessing to the one who reads for others and to any who "listen to its message and obey what it says."

REFLECT

The reference to the "one who reads" indicates that someone read it to a local assembly. Now there are many copies of the letter so it is not as necessary to have a reader for others.

RESPOND

With a friend, look at verse 3 and determine that the more you learn about the future the more you will be motivated to live a life glorifying to the Lord Jesus Christ.

WEEK 1: REVELATION 1

DAY 3

RECEIVE

Revelation 1:4–5

⁴ This letter is from John to the seven churches in the province of Asia. Grace and peace to you from the one who is, who always was, and who is still to come; from the sevenfold Spirit before his throne; ⁵ and from Jesus Christ. He is the faithful witness to these things, the first to rise from the dead, and the ruler of all the kings of the world. All glory to him who loves us and has freed us from our sins by shedding his blood for us.

The "sevenfold Spirit" seems to refer to the sevenfold character, or perfection, of the Holy Spirit. John was directing the letter to the seven churches in Asia Minor, now western Turkey. He pronounces peace from the eternal God, the Holy Spirit and the Lord Jesus Christ. John refers to Jesus as a faithful witness, the resurrected Christ and the ultimate ruler of the kings of the world. He then breaks into a doxology of praise for the Lord Jesus for what He has done by shedding His blood on Calvary.

REFLECT

Think of how grateful you can be that Jesus died for you to free you from your sins by shedding His blood on Calvary. As the apostle Paul wrote in Ephesians 1:3, "all praise to God."

RESPOND

Consider that Jesus is the ultimate ruler of world leaders by reading Psalm 2:1–12 and Proverbs 21:1. With your friend, focus on the fact that you serve a holy and sovereign God who is in control.

REVELATION

DAY 4

RECEIVE

Revelation 1:6-7

⁶ He has made us a Kingdom of priests for God his Father. All glory and power to him forever and ever! Amen. ⁷ Look! He comes with the clouds of heaven. And everyone will see him—even those who pierced him. And all the nations of the world will mourn for him. Yes! Amen!

These verses refer to the return of Jesus Christ to the earth. Previously the apostle Paul had written in 1 Thessalonians 4:13-18 about Church-age believers being caught up to meet Jesus in the air. He did not come to the earth at that time, but He will in the future and everyone will see Him. The reason all nations will mourn is that He comes as Judge and King. They dread His coming but believers welcome it.

REFLECT

Think of the difference for believers and unbelievers as they think about the Lord's return. It will be an occasion of blessing for believers but a time of judgment for unbelievers.

RESPOND

Talk with your disciple about the need to be ready to meet Jesus when He returns in the air. Later, after the seven-year Tribulation Jesus talked about in Matthew 24 and 25, those believers saved during the Tribulation will rejoice to see Him. Most of them, however, will die for their faith.

DAY 5

RECEIVE

Revelation 1:8

⁸ "I am the Alpha and the Omega—the beginning and the end," says the Lord God. "I am the one who is, who always was, and who is still to come—the Almighty One."

Alpha and Omega refer to the first and last letters of the Greek alphabet. It assumes Jesus is also everything in between. The verse also reveals the eternality of Jesus: He is, always was, and still is to come. He is the "Almighty one." This name first appears in Genesis 17:1-2 when God revealed Himself to Abraham as El-Shaddai—God Almighty. He has power over all.

REFLECT

Think of what a powerful God you serve. He has created the universe and yet can live in your heart when you trust Him as Savior.

RESPOND

Read John 14:16-17 and 17:22-23. These verses reveal that the godhead—although everywhere present—indwells individual believers. May the characteristics of the Holy Spirit, the Father and the Son be seen in your life.

WEEK 2: REVELATION 1

RECEIVE

DAY 1

Revelation 1:9

⁹ I, John, am your brother and your partner in suffering and in God's Kingdom and in the patient endurance to which Jesus calls us. I was exiled to the island of Patmos for preaching the word of God and for my testimony about Jesus.

John now described himself and where he was and why he was there. He was suffering as other believers were and was in patient endurance. Those statements together are significant. His location was the Island of Patmos. This was located in the Aegean Sea. This was southwest of Ephesus between Asia Minor (western Turkey) and Greece. He was exiled there because of preaching the gospel and telling about Jesus.

REFLECT

Have you suffered for the gospel and had others push you aside? If so, may God use you eventually, to use your testimony for Jesus in an even greater way.

RESPOND

With a friend, try to imagine what it must have been like for the apostle John. He was one of the closest disciples to the Lord Jesus and a Christian leader now exiled to an island. Early church fathers think this was in the rule of Domitian (about A.D. 96). The Roman Empire was not a friend of the gospel of the Lord Jesus Christ.

REVELATION

DAY 2

RECEIVE

Revelation 1:10-11

¹⁰ It was the Lord's Day, and I was worshiping in the Spirit. Suddenly, I heard behind me a loud voice like a trumpet blast. ¹¹ It said, "Write in a book everything you see, and send it to the seven churches in the cities of Ephesus, Smyrna, Pergamum, Thyatira, Sardis, Philadelphia, and Laodicea."

John records what he was doing when suddenly he heard a voice like a trumpet blast telling him what to do. In John's day they wrote on scrolls, although the Greek word involved is *biblion,* from which the word "book" is derived. John was to write everything he will see and is to send it to the seven churches in Asia Minor. The churches are specified so there is no mistaking the target audience of the original message in Revelation. It is now available for all believers to read.

REFLECT

Think of the privilege now of having a book to hold in your hands instead of a scroll that would need to be unrolled as you read. Also think of the advancement now to see books electronically. There are many ways for believers to proclaim the gospel that the early believers did not have.

RESPOND

Help your disciple to find a map that will show the location of these seven churches in Revelation. If you have access to a Bible dictionary, see what it says about these churches as each one is referred to in future verses.

WEEK 2: REVELATION 1

DAY 3

RECEIVE

Revelation 1:12-13

¹² When I turned to see who was speaking to me, I saw seven gold lampstands. ¹³ And standing in the middle of the lampstands was someone like the Son of Man. He was wearing a long robe with a gold sash across his chest.

There are many symbols in the book of Revelation. If one keeps reading, however, those symbols are sometimes explained, and that it true of the "gold lampstands." At this point it leaves one wondering. The "Son of Man" is an expression that Jesus used of Himself. It is used six times in Matthew 24 and 25 that tell about the great time of trouble to come on the earth that will be told about in Revelation 4 through 19.

REFLECT

What do you think was John's reaction when he saw this vision of the Lord Jesus Christ? You will be told later in the text. This is another indication to keep reading when you have questions.

RESPOND

With your friend, read Isaiah 11:1-5 that tells about the return of Jesus to set up His kingdom on earth. If you do not think this refers to His kingdom on earth, read verses 6-9.

REVELATION

DAY 4

RECEIVE

Revelation 1:14-16

¹⁴ His head and his hair were white like wool, as white as snow. And his eyes were like flames of fire. ¹⁵ His feet were like polished bronze refined in a furnace, and his voice thundered like mighty ocean waves. ¹⁶ He held seven stars in his right hand, and a sharp two-edged sword came from his mouth. And his face was like the sun in all its brilliance.

The apostle John continued to describe the appearance of the Son of Man. Some see His hair to picture the Ancient of Days, prophesied by Daniel (see Daniel 7:9). He held "seven stars" in his right hand. To whom does this refer? Again, the same answer: keep reading. Hebrews 4:12 tells about the two-edged sword, which is the Word of God. Jesus was able to speak worlds into existence and, as seen later in Revelation, He will be able to speak armies out of existence.

REFLECT

By having a copy of the Bible, you have a two-edged sword, which is the Word of God. In John 1:1 and 1:14 you see that Jesus is the Word who took on human flesh to dwell among mankind. As the Word, He is the expression of God.

RESPOND

Talk with your disciple about the spiritual warfare believers are engaged in today and the need to put on the armor of God mentioned in Ephesians 6:13-17. Notice especially the need to take the "sword of the Spirit, which is the word of God."

WEEK 2: REVELATION 1

DAY 5

RECEIVE

Revelation 1:17-18

¹⁷ When I saw him, I fell at his feet as if I were dead. But he laid his right hand on me and said, "Don't be afraid! I am the First and the Last. ¹⁸ I am the living one. I died, but look—I am alive forever and ever! And I hold the keys of death and the grave."

You no longer have to wonder how John reacted when he saw the vision of the Lord Jesus Christ. He prostrated himself at the feet of Jesus as if he were dead. Jesus told him not to be afraid and referred to Himself as "the First and the Last." This is the title of Jehovah, and reveals Jesus is Jehovah. Those who deny this do not accept the Word of God by what it says and means.

REFLECT

Is it new to you to consider Jesus is Jehovah? Modern English translations usually put LORD in all caps to show it refers to Jehovah. Compare Isaiah 44:6 and 48:12 with Revelation 1:17-18.

RESPOND

The two of you should study more about references to Jehovah and Jesus. Compare Isaiah 40:3 with John 1:23. John the Baptist referred to Isaiah 40:3 for what he was doing for Jesus.

WEEK 3: REVELATION 1, 2

DAY 1

RECEIVE

Revelation 1:19

[19] "Write down what you have seen—both the things that are now happening and the things that will happen."

This verse is considered by many to be the divine outline of the book of Revelation. The apostle John was to write three things: 1) what you have seen; 2) things that are now happening; and 3) things that will happen. Number 1) has to do with chapter 1; Number 2) has to do with chapters 2 and 3; and Number 3) has to do with chapters 4 and following.

REFLECT

Think of key passages in Bible books to help you know what to look for in the book. In John's gospel he gave the key in John 20:30-31. The key to the book of Acts is likely 1:8 that tells how the gospel was to be spread.

RESPOND

Talk with your friend about examining the book of Revelation with the outline of 1:19 in mind.

DAY 2

RECEIVE

Revelation 1:20

[20] "This is the meaning of the mystery of the seven stars you saw in my right hand and the seven gold lampstands: The seven stars are the angels of the seven churches, and the seven lampstands are the seven churches."

A "mystery" is something not previously revealed but is now made known. Remember about wondering in verse 12 about the "gold lampstands"? Here is the answer: it is the seven churches that are to give light in the world. In verse 16 the seven stars were mentioned. Here it is learned they are the "angels" of the seven churches. The Greek word "angel" means "messenger." One must determine whether it is a supernatural being or human. Some believe it is the pastor, but in the first century they did not have pastors as we do today. There were elders who led the churches, and their qualifications are given in 1 Timothy 3.

REFLECT

Consider this reminder as you read further in Revelation. Not every symbol is explained but many are.

RESPOND

Talk with your disciple about the fact that whether the "angel" (messenger) is a supernatural one or human, the messages to the seven churches are particularly given to the people in each. The messages should be read today with interest to see what applies to the present condition in some churches.

WEEK 3: REVELATION 1, 2

DAY 3

RECEIVE

Revelation 2:1

¹ "Write this letter to the angel of the church in Ephesus. This is the message from the one who holds the seven stars in his right hand, the one who walks among the seven gold lampstands:"

The Lord Jesus Christ first addressed the church in Ephesus. All seven of these churches were local churches, but the lessons drawn from them apply to churches today. Notice the description of the Lord Jesus is something said about Him in chapter 1. The message is from the Lord Jesus and is to be taken seriously.

REFLECT

Think about Jesus walking with a church. He is with the believers through all their persecutions and blessings. He walks among all the churches.

RESPOND

Talk with your friend about the nearness of Jesus to believers. Read John 16:33 to see He gives peace in the midst of trouble.

DAY 4

RECEIVE

Revelation 2:2-3

² "I know all the things you do. I have seen your hard work and your patient endurance. I know you don't tolerate evil people. You have examined the claims of those who say they are apostles but are not. You have discovered they are liars. ³ You have patiently suffered for me without quitting."

It is customary in these letters to the seven churches that something is said to commend them, except for the last church, Laodicea. The apostle Paul had spent three years in Ephesus where he had what some consider his greatest ministry. Jesus says several things that those in the church could be commended for. One could ask if local churches today are as concerned about these matters.

REFLECT

What are you doing in your local assembly to see that the group is doing things that can be commended by the Lord Jesus?

RESPOND

With your disciple, read Acts 19:8-10 and more of the chapter if you have time. This gives a background for Paul's ministry in Ephesus and the region. Ephesus was an important city on the western edge of Asia Minor (Turkey) where many worshiped the goddess Diana.

WEEK 3: REVELATION 1, 2

DAY 5

RECEIVE

Revelation 2:4-6

⁴ "But I have this complaint against you. You don't love me or each other as you did at first! ⁵ Look how far you have fallen! Turn back to me and do the works you did at first. If you don't repent, I will come and remove your lampstand from its place among the churches. ⁶ But this is in your favor: You hate the evil deeds of the Nicolaitans, just as I do."

After commending the church, Jesus then tells of a complaint about the group. They had left their first love. Jesus wanted them to repent (change their minds) about this condition. If they would not, He said He would remove their church from among the seven churches. Apart from this, it was in their favor that they hated the works of the Nicolaitans even as He did. There is uncertainty about this group, but they are also mentioned in the message to the church in Pergamum with some more details.

REFLECT

How is it with you now in comparison to when you first trusted in Jesus as Savior? Do you hunger to know more about the Bible as you did then? Have you grown in your love for Jesus because of what He has done for you?

RESPOND

Talk with your disciple about how things are going for you now in your Christian journey in comparison to when you first became believers. Determine to refresh your hearts by thinking of what Jesus has done for you. Decide to read more about Him in the Bible. Agree to be engaged in the Bible at least four times a week.

WEEK 4: REVELATION 2

DAY 1

RECEIVE

Revelation 2:7

⁷ "Anyone with ears to hear must listen to the Spirit and understand what he is saying to the churches. To everyone who is victorious I will give fruit from the tree of life in the paradise of God."

This is the appeal of Jesus for the churches to pay attention and understand what the Holy Spirit is saying. There is a promise to all who are "victorious" or an "overcomer." One is not awarded salvation by being an overcomer, but one becomes an overcomer by being born again in the family of God. The promise of the future is for eternal abundance in heaven.

REFLECT

Think about how God makes you a victorious person, or an overcomer, by believing in Jesus as your Savior.

RESPOND

With your friend, read 1 John 5:4-5. These verses help you to understand who is a victorious believer or an overcomer and can win the battle against the world. Thank the Lord for this.

DAY 2

RECEIVE

Revelation 2:8

⁸ "Write this letter to the angel of the church of Smyrna. This is the message from the one who is the First and the Last, who was dead but is now alive:"

Smyrna was about 35 miles north of Ephesus. It was a suffering church. Here a reference is made to the vision of Jesus seen by John in Revelation 1:17-18. The gospel message is that the eternal Son of God took on human flesh, died on the cross, was placed in a grave, and rose from the dead on the third day. These words must have comforted those facing martyrdom and had friends who had died for their faith in Jesus.

REFLECT

Think of those who have given their lives for their faith in Jesus. You may be in an area where that is the danger. Pray for such people and thank God who gave His only Son for you.

RESPOND

With your friend, consider that Jesus is all you need; indicated by the fact He is the First and the Last and everything in between. He was dead but is alive. Of all the past religious leaders, only the grave of the Lord Jesus Christ is empty.

DAY 3

RECEIVE

Revelation 2:9

⁹ "I know about your suffering and your poverty—but you are rich! I know the blasphemy of those opposing you. They say they are Jews, but they are not, because their synagogue belongs to Satan."

How comforting it must have been for the suffering saints in the church of Smyrna to realize the Lord knew every detail about their suffering and poverty. "But you are rich," the Lord told them. Their riches were not in the wealth of the world but in their possessions in Jesus. Some persecuting them claimed to be Jews but they were really of the synagogue of Satan.

REFLECT

Some are religious and think they serve God by persecuting those who believe in Jesus as the only way of salvation. Their problem is they are trusting in the works of their religion rather than trusting in Jesus who offers salvation by grace through faith.

RESPOND

With your disciple, read Romans 2:28-29 to see who the apostle Paul said was a true Jew. Talk together about how those today are only genuine "Christians" who have trusted in Jesus by grace through faith in Him.

DAY 4

RECEIVE

Revelation 2:10

[10] "Don't be afraid of what you are about to suffer. The devil will throw some of you into prison to test you. You will suffer for ten days. But if you remain faithful even when facing death, I will give you the crown of life."

"Don't be afraid of what you are about to suffer." What sobering words these are. Although their suffering will be for a relative short time in comparison to eternity, they are promised the crown of life as martyrs. The crown promised is a victor's crown for those who have faced persecution and suffering.

REFLECT

Think of the rewards Jesus will someday give those who have faithfully served Him on earth and some who have given their lives for Him. Make it your desire to honor Jesus in all you do.

RESPOND

The "crown of life" seems to be the same as mentioned in James 1:12 and 1 Peter 5:4. Talk with your friend about anything suffered on earth will be far more compensated by rewards in heaven.

WEEK 4: REVELATION 2

DAY 5

RECEIVE

Revelation 2:11

¹¹ "Anyone with ears to hear must listen to the Spirit and understand what he is saying to the churches. Whoever is victorious will not be harmed by the second death."

Here the exhortation is again made to listen and understand what the Spirit was saying to the churches (not just to the church of Smyrna). Those who have believed in Jesus are the victorious ones and will not be harmed by the second death. The "second death" is a reference to what unbelievers will experience when they are cast into the lake of fire.

REFLECT

Thank God that by trusting in Jesus as Savior you will avoid eternal condemnation.

RESPOND

With your disciple, discuss the warning to escape condemnation. See such verses as John 3:16-18. For a reference to the "second death" see Revelation 20:11-15 that describes what everyone who has rejected Jesus as Savior will face.

WEEK 5: REVELATION 2

DAY 1

RECEIVE

Revelation 2:12

[12] "Write this letter to the angel of the church in Pergamum. This is the message from the one with the sharp two-edged sword:"

The church in Pergamum was about 45 miles north of Smyrna. This description of Jesus is found in Revelation 1:16. The two-edged sword was in His mouth, and by it He could speak the universe into existence and armies out of existence. As the "Word" in John 1:1, the Lord Jesus was the expression of God. John 1:14 tells us the "Word became human and made his home among us."

REFLECT

Think of the power in the tongue of the Lord, described as a two-edged sword. No one else has such great power and authority.

RESPOND

With your disciple, read Revelation 19:15 to see how Jesus, at His Second Coming to earth, will strike down the nations with the sword that comes from His mouth.

REVELATION

DAY 2

RECEIVE

Revelation 2:13

¹³ "I know that you live in the city where Satan has his throne, yet you have remained loyal to me. You refused to deny me even when Antipas, my faithful witness, was martyred among you there in Satan's city."

Pergamum was a key center for cult worship, including emperor worship. No wonder it could be said that Satan had his throne there because he was dominating the area. Those in the church had remained faithful to the Lord Jesus and had not denied their Lord and Savior. This was in spite of one of their own being martyred, perhaps for not being willing to worship the emperor.

REFLECT

Have the difficulties and persecution of other believers caused you to stand stronger for your faith? That is the testimony of some who have experienced such.

RESPOND

Talk with your friend about where you live today. Although not the same as Pergamum, there is the worship of other gods in your midst. It may only be the god of materialism, but that is an idol if it comes between you and God. Read Matthew 6:24 to see one cannot serve two masters.

WEEK 5: REVELATION 2

DAY 3

RECEIVE

Revelation 2:14-15

¹⁴ "But I have a few complaints against you. You tolerate some among you whose teaching is like that of Balaam, who showed Balak how to trip up the people of Israel. He taught them to sin by eating food offered to idols and by committing sexual sin. ¹⁵ In a similar way, you have some Nicolaitans among you who follow the same teaching."

After commending the church of Pergamum, Jesus now had some complaints against them. The mention of the Nicolaitans gives additional insight into what their heresy was about, also mentioned by name in the complaint against the church of Ephesus in 2:6. Balaam had taught Israel to compromise with immorality and idolatry. Hypocrisy and compromise should never be the characteristics of believers.

REFLECT

Have there been times you have compromised what you believe because of pressure from friends? What will you do the next time such temptation comes?

RESPOND

With your disciple, read 1 Corinthians 8:1-13 to see the Corinthian believers were also struggling with eating food offered to idols and the bad testimony it was.

REVELATION

DAY 4

RECEIVE

Revelation 2:16

¹⁶ "Repent of your sin, or I will come to you suddenly and fight against them with the sword of my mouth."

Jesus exhorts those in Pergamum to repent (change their minds) about their sin. If not, He would come to them and bring judgment by the sword of His mouth. Believers have eternal life if they believe in Jesus for salvation (see John 3:16). God disciplines believers, however, for dishonoring Him. Discipline by an earthly parent is the sign of love and ownership of a child; God also does this with His own.

REFLECT

Read Hebrews 12:7-11 and discuss with your friend what the passage says about God's chastening.

RESPOND

Talk with your friend about any chastening experienced as a result of dishonoring God. Be honest with each other and gain strength by realizing it is a common experience and believers need to support each other at such times.

WEEK 5: REVELATION 2

DAY 5

RECEIVE

Revelation 2:17

¹⁷ "Anyone with ears to hear must listen to the Spirit and understand what he is saying to the churches. To everyone who is victorious I will give some of the manna that has been hidden away in heaven. And I will give to each one a white stone, and on the stone will be engraved a new name that no one understands except the one who receives it."

"Anyone" refers to everybody reading or hearing this message. The manna from heaven had to do with spiritual sustenance. Jesus referred to Himself as the "living bread that came down from heaven" (John 6:51). It is doubtful what is meant by the white stone, but the main thing is it indicated approval. Sometimes used in legal cases, other times at athletic contests, even as an indication of welcoming guests. Jesus will someday welcome all believers to His home.

REFLECT

Is it your desire to please Jesus in all you do regardless of the cost? This will honor the One who gave His life for you.

RESPOND

Discuss with your friend what you have learned from the message to the church in Pergamum. What lessons for the Christian life does it give you?

WEEK 6: REVELATION 2

DAY 1

RECEIVE

Revelation 2:18

[18] "Write this letter to the angel of the church in Thyatira. This is the message from the Son of God, whose eyes are like flames of fire, whose feet are like polished bronze."

Thyatira was about 40 miles southeast of Pergamum. Thyatira was known for its trade guilds and dyeing industry. The description of the Lord Jesus is similar to that mentioned in 1:13-15. Previously He was referred to as the Son of Man; here He is called the Son of God. His eyes like flames of fire and His feet of bronze refer to severe judgment that was about to be pronounced on the church in Thyatira.

REFLECT

Think of the Lord Jesus whom you serve. He is a God of love because He gave His life for lost humanity. He is also a God of judgment to those who refuse to accept the pardon He offers and dishonor Him with their lives.

RESPOND

With your disciple, read Acts 16:11-15 to see the comments about Lydia from Thyatira. Pray that God will open the hearts of your friends to hear the gospel as He opened Lydia's heart to hear what Paul had to present.

DAY 2

RECEIVE

Revelation 2:19

¹⁹ "I know all the things you do. I have seen your love, your faith, your service, and your patient endurance. And I can see your constant improvement in all these things."

The believers in Thyatira would be sobered to realize that Jesus knew "all things" they were doing. Jesus commended them for their love, faith, service and patient endurance. This list is impressive, but even more so is that they were constantly improving in these qualities. One could not expect any greater commendation.

REFLECT

Think of these four qualities the Lord singled out for which to commend the believers in Thyatira. How would you do in each category? Think of what you could do to improve.

RESPOND

You and your friend need to talk about how you are doing with showing love, faith, service and patient endurance. Discuss what you could do to improve in each area.

WEEK 6: REVELATION 2

RECEIVE

DAY 3

Revelation 2:20-21

[20] "But I have this complaint against you. You are permitting that woman—that Jezebel who calls herself a prophet—to lead my servants astray. She teaches them to commit sexual sin and to eat food offered to idols. [21] I gave her time to repent, but she does not want to turn away from her immorality."

After giving great commendation to the church of Thyatira, Jesus now rebuked them. Apparently they had the ability not to permit Jezebel to be a false prophet in their midst. But they were permitting her to lead servants of Christ astray and even to teach them to commit sin. She had led them into immorality and idol worship. Jesus had given her time to repent, but she was unwilling to do so.

REFLECT

Think of God's willingness to give people time to repent; that is, to change their minds, about sinful behavior and the need to turn to Him.

RESPOND

To show from the Scriptures God's willingness to have people repent and that all immorality is contrary to His will, read 2 Peter 3:9 and 1 Thessalonians 4:3.

REVELATION

DAY 4

RECEIVE

Revelation 2:22-23

²² "Therefore, I will throw her on a bed of suffering, and those who commit adultery with her will suffer greatly unless they repent and turn away from her evil deeds. ²³ I will strike all her children dead. Then all the churches will know that I am the one who searches out the thoughts and intentions of every person. And I will give to each of you whatever you deserve."

This is God's punishment for Jezebel and all who practice adultery with her—unless they repent. God was still inviting them to change their minds about their evil activities and the need to turn to Him. God reminds all the churches—and those today—that He knows the thoughts and intentions of every person. And each one will receive what is deserved.

REFLECT

Does this cause you to think more seriously about the evil around you and that someday God will judge those involved?

RESPOND

With your friend, read Hebrews 4:11-13 where we are told about the power of the Word of God and how it exposes one's thoughts and intentions.

WEEK 6: REVELATION 2

DAY 5

RECEIVE

Revelation 2:24-26

²⁴ "But I also have a message for the rest of you in Thyatira who have not followed this false teaching ('deeper truths,' as they call them—depths of Satan, actually). I will ask nothing more of you ²⁵ except that you hold tightly to what you have until I come. ²⁶ To all who are victorious, who obey me to the very end, to them I will give authority over all the nations."

It seems in every age there is a remnant of people who remain faithful to God. They had not believed in the mystery religion of those who had followed Jezebel. All that is asked is that they remain faithful to the Lord Jesus. Those who are victorious are promised authority over all nations. This will be fulfilled during the 1000-year reign of Jesus on earth.

REFLECT

Think of the rewards you will have by being faithful in following the Lord Jesus and not being sidetracked into counterfeit religious groups.

RESPOND

To be reminded of an overcoming Christian, read 1 John 5:4. To see a reference to ruling over nations, read Revelation 20:6 to see the promise to believers in Jesus.

Week 7: Revelation 2, 3

RECEIVE

DAY 1

Revelation 2:27-29

²⁷ "They will rule the nations with an iron rod and smash them like clay pots. ²⁸ They will have the same authority I received from my Father, and I will also give them the morning star! ²⁹ Anyone with ears to hear must listen to the Spirit and understand what he is saying to the churches."

Having told the faithful believers in Thyatira that Jesus would give them authority over all the nations, here they are told they will rule with an iron rod and destroy them. As the morning star appears before sunrise, some believe this is a reference to the rapture occurring before the return of Jesus to the earth. The appeal to Thyatira ends with urging everyone to listen and understand what the Holy Spirit is saying to the churches.

REFLECT

Has this portion of Scripture encouraged you to see the authority believers in Jesus will have in the future and the need to honor Him now in daily living?

RESPOND

With your disciple, read Revelation 22:16 that refers to Jesus calling Himself the "bright morning star." Talk together about what you have learned from the message to the church at Thyatira.

REVELATION

DAY 2

RECEIVE

Revelation 3:1

¹ "Write this letter to the angel of the church in Sardis. This is the message from the one who has the sevenfold Spirit of God and the seven stars: I know all the things you do, and that you have a reputation for being alive—but you are dead."

Sardis was about 30 miles southeast of Thyatira. The "sevenfold Spirit of God" is also mentioned in 1:4. It is likely a reference to all the aspects of the Holy Spirit. Isaiah 11:2 is similar to this expression. The "seven stars" is defined in 1:20 as the angels (messengers) of the seven churches. Sardis was a wealthy city but was spiritually corrupt. Others thought they were alive but they were really spiritually dead.

REFLECT

Have you sometimes been deceived by appearances? Some may seem to be spiritually alive, but are they only going along with a Christian crowd?

RESPOND

Read 1 Samuel 16:6-13 to see from David's life that the Lord looks at the heart more than the appearance.

WEEK 7: REVELATION 2, 3

DAY 3

RECEIVE

Revelation 3:2-3

² "Wake up! Strengthen what little remains, for even what is left is almost dead. I find that your actions do not meet the requirements of my God. ³ Go back to what you heard and believed at first; hold to it firmly. Repent and turn to me again. If you don't wake up, I will come to you suddenly, as unexpected as a thief."

There was a little life left in the church in Sardis so the Lord urges them to strengthen what was left. The actions of believers there did not measure up to the standards of God. Similar to what was told the church of Ephesus, these people had seemed to have left their first love. If they didn't change the direction in their lives, the Lord would unexpectedly come and bring judgment.

REFLECT

Again, think of your life. Have you been following Jesus for more than a year? If so, does your heart still burn with the same passion for Him and the Scriptures as it did when you first believed?

RESPOND

An accident or any cause of sudden death can snap a person into eternity. Use this realization in witnessing and ask if the person is ready for eternity when that time comes. Use 2 Corinthians 6:2 to emphasize that "today is the day of salvation." No one can be sure of tomorrow.

RECEIVE

DAY 4

Revelation 3:4-5

⁴ "Yet there are some in the church in Sardis who have not soiled their clothes with evil. They will walk with me in white, for they are worthy. ⁵ All who are victorious will be clothed in white. I will never erase their names from the Book of Life, but I will announce before my Father and his angels that they are mine."

Commendation was given for the faithful yet in Sardis. The reference to walking with the Lord in white reminds one of Revelation 19:8 that says the fine linen clean and bright is the righteous acts of the saints. The names of these in Sardis will never be erased from the Book of Life. Those who believe in Jesus have everlasting (eternal) life. Jesus is pleased to announce before the heavenly Father and the angels that they are "mine."

REFLECT

If you have trusted in Jesus as your Savior, think how pleased you can be that you are secure in His love. He is pleased to call you His own.

RESPOND

For verses that tell you and your friend about the security believers have in Jesus, see John 3:16; 5:24; and 10:28-29. Are you living in a way that shows thankfulness and that promotes God's glory for what He has done for you?

DAY 5

RECEIVE

Revelation 3:6

⁶ "Anyone with ears to hear must listen to the Spirit and understand what he is saying to the churches."

As before, this message is given to all the churches: everyone needs to listen and understand what Jesus is saying to them. There are both items of commendation and warnings. Many are religious but relatively few are born again by believing in Jesus' finished work on the cross. Only those relying on a relationship with Jesus rather than on a religion or a church truly have security.

REFLECT

How is it with you? Hopefully you are thankful for the church you attend, but are you relying on it or the Lord Jesus to bring assurance of eternal life? Religion is man's attempt to reach up to God; Christianity is God reaching down to mankind.

RESPOND

With your disciple, read again these six verses that tell about the message of Jesus to the church in Sardis. What lessons can be learned for today?

WEEK 8: REVELATION 3

DAY 1

RECEIVE

Revelation 3:7

⁷ "Write this letter to the angel of the church in Philadelphia. This is the message from the one who is holy and true, the one who has the key of David. What he opens, no one can close; and what he closes, no one can open:"

Philadelphia was about 28 miles southeast of Sardis. The Greek words that are the basis of the name mean "brotherly love" and likely came from two earthly Roman rulers who loved each other. The Lord Jesus has the key of David and spoke to the church in Philadelphia. He is holy and true and has all power. The promise to believers is that when Jesus opens, no one is able to close, and when He closes no one can open. That can also apply to opportunities to spread the gospel.

REFLECT

Think of the opportunities God provides for you to tell others about Jesus. When He opens the door, no one can shut it.

RESPOND

With your friend, read what the apostle Paul wrote in Philippians 1:12-14 about his imprisonment resulting in a furtherance of the gospel. Even pandemics cannot prevent the gospel from being spread to others. Are you doing what you can to tell others about Jesus no matter your circumstances? Do you want to disciple the lost at any cost?

DAY 2

RECEIVE

Revelation 3:8-9

⁸ "I know all the things you do, and I have opened a door for you that no one can close. You have little strength, yet you obeyed my word and did not deny me. ⁹ Look, I will force those who belong to Satan's synagogue—those liars who say they are Jews but are not—to come and bow down at your feet. They will acknowledge that you are the ones I love."

The Lord made His message personal to those in the church in Philadelphia. His promise before about opening and shutting of doors was general, now it was specific. Those in this church had little strength but they had remained faithful. Unbelieving Jews were persecuting those who loved Jesus, but they would someday admit that those in the church were those Jesus loved.

REFLECT

Even though you feel you have little strength to serve the Lord, can you be like the Philadelphian believers and obey the Lord and not deny Him?

RESPOND

What kind of Jews could be referred to in this passage? They could be like Saul of Tarsus, also later known as the apostle Paul. During his unsaved days he persecuted Christ followers (read Acts 22:3-5). When will unbelievers someday admit Jesus is Lord and will acknowledge His followers? With your friend read Philippians 2:5-11 to see what it says about Jesus. People will either bow to Jesus in this life or later in the afterlife.

WEEK 8: REVELATION 3

DAY 3

RECEIVE

Revelation 3:10

¹⁰ "Because you have obeyed my command to persevere, I will protect you from the great time of testing that will come upon the whole world to test those who belong to this world."

The believers in the church in Philadelphia had obeyed Jesus' command to persevere. The promise He made to that church—and to all believers—is that He would keep them from the "great time of testing that would come upon the whole world." This verse is debated by those who discuss end-time events. Some think the Church, the Body of Christ, will pass through the 70th Week of Daniel, known as the Tribulation but will be kept from testing. Others point out, however, that the promise is not to be kept from the testing but to be kept from even the time of testing. This would argue for the rapture of 1 Thessalonians 4:13-18 to occur before the seven-year Tribulation.

REFLECT

Whatever your understanding of future events is, do you have confidence that God will honor you for obeying Him?

RESPOND

As we will see in future chapters of Revelation, many believers will die for their faith by refusing to receive the mark of the beast. Even today, before these prophetic events occur, many are dying for their faith in Jesus as Savior. With your friend, pray for those suffering persecution because of believing in Jesus.

REVELATION

RECEIVE

DAY 4

Revelation 3:11-12

[11] "I am coming soon. Hold on to what you have, so that no one will take away your crown. [12] All who are victorious will become pillars in the Temple of my God, and they will never have to leave it. And I will write on them the name of my God, and they will be citizens in the city of my God—the new Jerusalem that comes down from heaven from my God. And I will also write on them my new name."

The reference to coming "soon" means "quickly" or "suddenly." Those with a confidence in the Lord's return are encouraged to hold on to what they have. The "crown" referred to is a "victor's crown." Various names will be written on believers that will reveal ownership and pleasure of the owner—the eternal God. How all this will be done is uncertain, but the followers of Jesus can know everything will be done perfectly because Jesus is a perfect Savior.

REFLECT

Even though there are many things in the Bible you may not understand, do you have confidence in your perfect Savior to make everything perfect?

RESPOND

Believers often wonder what it will be like in heaven. Not many specifics are revealed, but one thing is certain: believers will be with Jesus. With your friend, read John 14:1-3 to be reassured that believers will be with Jesus.

WEEK 8: REVELATION 3

DAY 5

RECEIVE

Revelation 3:13

¹³ "Anyone with ears to hear must listen to the Spirit and understand what he is saying to the churches."

Although this is similar to what is said to each church, notice it is addressed to all the churches at that time. Some believe the seven churches of Revelation are a prediction of what the Church age will be like from Pentecost (see Acts 2) until the return of Jesus. It seems, however, the conditions in them are typical of local churches in all ages.

REFLECT

As you read about the church in Philadelphia, does it remind you of what you see in your local fellowship? If Jesus were to speak to your church group now, would He say similar things to you?

RESPOND

Talk with your friend about what would need to be done in your local fellowship to be able to hear the same comments Jesus made to the church in Philadelphia. Gentile believers would be in one body—the Church.

WEEK 9: REVELATION 3

DAY 1

RECEIVE

Revelation 3:14

[14] "Write this letter to the angel of the church in Laodicea. This is the message from the one who is the Amen—the faithful and true witness, the beginning of God's new creation:"

This is the last letter to the seven churches of Revelation 2 and 3. Laodicea was about 40 miles southeast of Philadelphia. The seven churches were in a geographical arc beginning with Ephesus and ending with Laodicea. Makes one wonder if they resembled a candelabra and that is why they were referred to as the seven lampstands in Revelation 1:20. The description of Jesus is similar to what is said in 1:5. Jesus is God and did not have a beginning, He is the beginning; He is the Creator.

REFLECT

Think of Jesus as the "Amen"; that is, He is the final word. His words are more authoritative than anyone else's.

RESPOND

With your disciple, read John 1:1-5 and Colossians 1:15-20 that speak of the role of the Lord Jesus Christ in creation. Others can speculate about creation, but believers in Christ know by revelation about the Origin of creation.

REVELATION

DAY 2

RECEIVE

Revelation 3:15-16

¹⁵ "I know all the things you do, that you are neither hot nor cold. I wish that you were one or the other! ¹⁶ But since you are like lukewarm water, neither hot nor cold, I will spit you out of my mouth!"

Jesus rebuked the church for being like lukewarm water that He wanted to spit out. The locals knew about lukewarm water that was sickening to drink. Jesus said that is what the church was like. The church people were neither hot nor cold spiritually; they were compromisers who would not take a position. Outsiders could not know whether they believed in the testimony of Jesus or not.

REFLECT

What do others see as they view your life? Do they see someone who is passionate to know more about Jesus and His Word? If this is not what they see, are they entitled to believe Jesus feels the same about you that He felt about the Laodicean church?

RESPOND

What should believers do if they are in a compromising church that refuses to take a stand for the Word of God? With your friend, read 2 Timothy 3:1-5 that instructs what to do in such a situation.

WEEK 9: REVELATION 3

DAY 3

RECEIVE

Revelation 3:17-19

[17] "You say, 'I am rich. I have everything I want. I don't need a thing!' And you don't realize that you are wretched and miserable and poor and blind and naked. [18] So I advise you to buy gold from me—gold that has been purified by fire. Then you will be rich. Also buy white garments from me so you will not be shamed by your nakedness, and ointment for your eyes so you will be able to see. [19] I correct and discipline everyone I love. So be diligent and turn from your indifference."

Laodicea was known for its wealth. The area made salve for the eyes and ears. Materialism was their God instead of Jehovah. They made eye salve but they were spiritually blind. They needed "white garments," which Revelation 19:8 says reveals the good deeds of God's people. Jesus disciplines those He loves so He told them to turn from being apathetic.

REFLECT

Although money is needed to supply one's needs, do you realize the risk of putting more trust in material belongings than in Jesus? Do you possess your possessions or do they possess you?

RESPOND

With your disciple, read Matthew 6:24 about money. Knowing that one cannot serve two masters has led some to leave counterfeit religious groups after growing in their knowledge about the Lord Jesus. How does it apply to you?

REVELATION

DAY 4

RECEIVE

Revelation 3:20-21

[20] "Look! I stand at the door and knock. If you hear my voice and open the door, I will come in, and we will share a meal together as friends. [21] Those who are victorious will sit with me on my throne, just as I was victorious and sat with my Father on his throne."

Many have seen the artist's painting of Jesus standing at the door, based on Revelation 3:20. There is no outside handle on the door so it must be opened from the inside. Jesus wanted those in the Laodicean church to open the door so He could have fellowship with them. They had shut Him out. Victorious believers would be welcomed to sit with Him on His throne.

REFLECT

Is your heart a welcoming one for Jesus? Do you fellowship with Him by reading the Scriptures and praying?

RESPOND

Do you and your friend consider yourselves friends of Jesus? Do you read about Him in the Bible and talk to Him in prayer the same way you talk to friends? If you have accepted His pardon for your sins the promise of 1 John 5:4-5 can be claimed by you. Read these verses and thank the Lord for what He has done for you.

WEEK 9: REVELATION 3

DAY 5

RECEIVE

Revelation 3:22

²² "Anyone with ears to hear must listen to the Spirit and understand what he is saying to the churches."

This is a final appeal to the seven churches of Revelation. These churches seem characteristic of churches that can be found in every age. There has been commendation for some of the churches but rebuke sometimes given along with the praise. This portion is included in the Bible to give examples of what should be watched for today. The messages should cause serious thought for believers.

REFLECT

As you think back over the messages to the seven churches, which one would best describe the group you attend? What can you do to improve the spiritual level of your fellowship?

RESPOND

Spend time with your disciple briefly glancing at the messages to these seven churches. Discuss which one or ones reflect what your group is like. Does it concern you that some could be with you in church who have never trusted in Jesus as Savior? That was the case with Judas who betrayed Jesus. The other disciples never suspected him of unbelief.

Week 10: Revelation 4

RECEIVE

DAY 1

Revelation 4:1

¹ Then as I looked, I saw a door standing open in heaven, and the same voice I had heard before spoke to me like a trumpet blast. The voice said, "Come up here, and I will show you what must happen after this."

The book of Revelation now comes to the third item of what John was told to write about. In Revelation 1:19, John was told to write about "what you have seen" (chapter 1); "the things that are now happening" (chapters 2 and 3); and "the things that will happen" (chapters 4 and following). The words "after this" reveal there is a change in subject as John was told, "I will show you what must happen after this." From here forward the church is never seen on earth.

REFLECT

Think how blessed you are to have a copy of Revelation to read about these events. You have read about the vision of Christ that John saw in chapter 1, and the messages to the seven churches in chapters 2 and 3. Now you will see what occurs "after this."

RESPOND

Do you have a friend to follow these comments about the book of Revelation? Many people are interested in Revelation so you should help someone learn more about the book.

DAY 2

RECEIVE

Revelation 4:2-4

² And instantly I was in the Spirit, and I saw a throne in heaven and someone sitting on it. ³ The one sitting on the throne was as brilliant as gemstones—like jasper and carnelian. And the glow of an emerald circled his throne like a rainbow. ⁴ Twenty-four thrones surrounded him, and twenty-four elders sat on them. They were all clothed in white and had gold crowns on their heads.

The apostle John was physically on earth but in spirit was taken into heaven. There he saw on a throne one with a majestic description. Surrounding this magnificent one were 24 thrones with 24 elders. It is unsure who the 24 were, but because they were clothed in white and had victors' crowns on their heads suggests they represented Church-age believers who had been previously raptured and rewarded in heaven.

REFLECT

Think of the struggle John had of describing a heavenly scene in language humans would understand. Think of the difficulty you would have had.

RESPOND

Remind your friend of the significance of the white clothing in heaven. Read Revelation 19:6-8 to see mention of the white linen at the great wedding feast. Read also 1 Corinthians 3:10-15 that tells about believers being rewarded for their service on earth for Jesus.

DAY 3

RECEIVE

Revelation 4:5-6

⁵ From the throne came flashes of lightning and the rumble of thunder. And in front of the throne were seven torches with burning flames. This is the sevenfold Spirit of God. ⁶ In front of the throne was a shiny sea of glass, sparkling like crystal. In the center and around the throne were four living beings, each covered with eyes, front and back.

What John saw coming from the throne was an indication of coming judgment. The "sevenfold Spirit" likely refers to the fullness or perfection of the Holy Spirit. John describes the sea of glass in front of the throne as "sparkling like crystal." The eyes of the four living beings reveal the possibility to see everything.

REFLECT

Think about the unimaginable majesty of the scene in heaven. Think also of the difficulty to describe it. Humans on earth have no way of comprehending such a scene.

RESPOND

Talk with your disciple about the concern that today we know little about what heaven is really like. We can be confident, however, that heaven will be a perfect place for all believers because Jesus, the perfect Son of God, is there.

RECEIVE

DAY 4

Revelation 4:7-8

⁷ The first of these living beings was like a lion; the second was like an ox; the third had a human face; and the fourth was like an eagle in flight. ⁸ Each of these living beings had six wings, and their wings were covered all over with eyes, inside and out. Day after day and night after night they keep on saying, "Holy, holy, holy is the Lord God, the Almighty—the one who always was, who is, and who is still to come."

The apostle John described what the four living beings were like. Bible commentators see a similarity to the four gospels in the description of these four beings. A lion, the king of all animals, they see reflected in the gospel of Matthew who presented Jesus as King. The ox, or calf, was a sacrificial animal and Mark presented Jesus as a Servant. The one with a human face reminds one of Luke who presented Jesus as the Son of Man. The eagle in flight reminds one of the gospel of John that presented Jesus as the Son of God. These living beings were praising God.

REFLECT

Do you praise God often? The living beings emphasized the holiness of God as they praised Him saying, "Holy, holy, holy is the Lord God, the Almighty."

RESPOND

With your friend, read Isaiah 6:1-6. The more Isaiah was aware of his unworthiness, the more he was impressed with God's holiness. May this be true for you and your friend.

WEEK 10: REVELATION 4

DAY 5

RECEIVE

Revelation 4:9-11

⁹ Whenever the living beings give glory and honor and thanks to the one sitting on the throne (the one who lives forever and ever), ¹⁰ the twenty-four elders fall down and worship the one sitting on the throne (the one who lives forever and ever). And they lay their crowns before the throne and say, ¹¹ "You are worthy, O Lord our God, to receive glory and honor and power. For you created all things, and they exist because you created what you pleased."

Verse 8 had referred to God as "the one who always was, who is, and who is still to come." Verses 9 and 10 each describe Him as "the one who lives forever and ever." The 24 elders lay their crowns before the throne and proclaim God's worthiness to "receive glory and honor and power." This is because He has "created all things," and they exist because He created what pleased Him.

REFLECT

Think of God who is powerful over all; that is, He is "Almighty." What a great God every believer in Jesus serves! May this fill your heart with praise for Him.

RESPOND

Talk with your disciple about some of the things that indicate the greatness of God. Think about the universe. Read Colossians 1:15-20 to read about the Lord Jesus Christ, the agent through whom God created everything. Jesus Christ is also head of the Church. Take time to praise Him in prayer.

WEEK 11: REVELATION 5

DAY 1

RECEIVE

Revelation 5:1–3

¹ Then I saw a scroll in the right hand of the one who was sitting on the throne. There was writing on the inside and the outside of the scroll, and it was sealed with seven seals. ² And I saw a strong angel, who shouted with a loud voice: "Who is worthy to break the seals on this scroll and open it?" ³ But no one in heaven or on earth or under the earth was able to open the scroll and read it.

In those days the writing was done on a scroll, not a book as it is thought of today. As each seal would be removed the contents of the scroll would be revealed. This scroll had seven seals. The search for someone worthy to open the seals was not found. No creature in heaven or on earth was able to open and read it.

REFLECT

Consider that Revelation 4 and 5 take place in heaven. Soon the focus will be on earth. Do you feel like a spectator sitting on the sidelines watching what is about to unfold?

RESPOND

Hopefully you have a friend to follow your study of Revelation. It is a principle that you need to pass on what you are learning. Read 2 Timothy 2:1-2 to see what the apostle Paul told Timothy about doing so.

RECEIVE

DAY 2

Revelation 5:4-5

⁴ Then I began to weep bitterly because no one was found worthy to open the scroll and read it. ⁵ But one of the twenty-four elders said to me, "Stop weeping! Look, the Lion of the tribe of Judah, the heir to David's throne, has won the victory. He is worthy to open the scroll and its seven seals."

The apostle John was heartbroken that no creature was found who was able to break open the seals of the scroll. One of the 24 elders urges John to stop weeping because the Lord Jesus Christ is worthy to do so. The Lord Jesus is described as "the Lion of the tribe of Judah, and the heir to David's throne." Prophecy had pointed to this member of the godhead who is holy and worthy to open the scroll.

REFLECT

Think how this passage reveals Jesus Christ is more worthy than any created being. He is the Creator so He is superior to anything and everyone He has created.

RESPOND

Revelation 5 is introducing what will eventually take place on earth as revealed in the scroll. It is fitting the Creator of the world is the one worthy to judge the world. He gave His life on the cross for mankind. Read John 1:10-13 to see what the apostle John wrote about Jesus' first coming.

WEEK 11: REVELATION 5

DAY 3

RECEIVE

Revelation 5:6-7

⁶ Then I saw a Lamb that looked as if it had been slaughtered, but it was now standing between the throne and the four living beings and among the twenty-four elders. He had seven horns and seven eyes, which represent the sevenfold Spirit of God that is sent out into every part of the earth. ⁷ He stepped forward and took the scroll from the right hand of the one sitting on the throne.

Verse 5 referred to Jesus as a "Lion" and now He is spoken of as a "Lamb." In Revelation, John used the word for "little lamb" 27 times and it is not used elsewhere in the New Testament. At His first advent Jesus came as a sacrificial lamb, but at His second advent He will come as a lion. The "seven horns" refer to power. The "seven eyes" to seeing everything. The "sevenfold Spirit" is a symbol of the Holy Spirit. This little lamb stepped forward and took the scroll from the one sitting on the throne.

REFLECT

Think about some of the majesties of heaven. John could not explain them exactly so he used symbolic language.

RESPOND

Read John 1:29-31 to see how John the Baptist referred to the one who had come to be the sacrificial lamb for sin. It is noteworthy that Jesus died on the cross during Passover, which was the time for the lamb to be sacrificed.

DAY 4

RECEIVE

Revelation 5:8-10

⁸ And when he took the scroll, the four living beings and the twenty-four elders fell down before the Lamb. Each one had a harp, and they held gold bowls filled with incense, which are the prayers of God's people. ⁹ And they sang a new song with these words: "You are worthy to take the scroll and break its seals and open it. For you were slaughtered, and your blood has ransomed people for God from every tribe and language and people and nation. ¹⁰ And you have caused them to become a Kingdom of priests for our God. And they will reign on the earth."

Worship is ascribed to the Lamb for what He had done for people. "Worship" is derived from an old English word "worthship." Any time one is thinking about God's worth, that is worship. This is true whether singing a hymn, reading the Scriptures, praying, or meditating. This passage is looking ahead to a future time when the events of Revelation will be fulfilled.

REFLECT

Spend time thinking about the worth of God. Know that in so doing you are worshiping Him. Some use a hymnbook during their devotional times. The lyrics can help lift your heart to God.

RESPOND

With your friend, look ahead to Revelation 8:3-4 to see incense associated with the prayers of God's people. Consider how your prayers make sweet incense to God. Read Psalm 141:1-2 in this regard.

WEEK 11: REVELATION 5

DAY 5

RECEIVE

Revelation 5:11-12

¹¹ Then I looked again, and I heard the voices of thousands and millions of angels around the throne and of the living beings and the elders. ¹² And they sang in a mighty chorus: "Worthy is the Lamb who was slaughtered—to receive power and riches and wisdom and strength and honor and glory and blessing."

The word "slaughtered" refers to a violent death. Because of what Jesus went through, millions of angels, along with the living beings and elders, sang a chorus of praise to Him. They acknowledged that He was worthy to receive power, riches, wisdom, strength, honor, glory and blessing.

REFLECT

Imagine this scene in heaven with all these created beings worshiping God. What they said the Savior was worthy of seems to cover all needs. In this sense, you can know that for all things spiritual, Jesus is all you need.

RESPOND

May you and your disciple spend time talking about God's worth, and in this way worshiping Him. Imagine what life in general and your life in particular would be like if Jesus had not died on the cross for you. Read Romans 15:5-6 to see what the apostle Paul said about praising God.

Week 12: Revelation 5, 6

RECEIVE

DAY 1

Revelation 5:13-14

¹³ And then I heard every creature in heaven and on earth and under the earth and in the sea. They sang: "Blessing and honor and glory and power belong to the one sitting on the throne and to the Lamb forever and ever." ¹⁴ And the four living beings said, "Amen!" And the twenty-four elders fell down and worshiped the Lamb.

This is a great picture of worship in heaven. The millions of angels, living beings and elders had worshiped in a similar way as seen in verses 11-12, now joining in are "every creature in heaven and on earth and under the earth and in the sea." People will either bow down and worship Jesus as the redeemer now or they will in eternity.

REFLECT

Hopefully these passages in Revelation will enable you to see more clearly the wonderful Lord and redeemer you have.

RESPOND

To see that all will someday bow down and worship the Lord, read Philippians 2:5-11. With fellow believers, rejoice in the God of your salvation now rather than having to do so later as an unbeliever.

REVELATION

DAY 2

RECEIVE

Revelation 6:1-2

¹ As I watched, the Lamb broke the first of the seven seals on the scroll. Then I heard one of the four living beings say with a voice like thunder, "Come!" ² I looked up and saw a white horse standing there. Its rider carried a bow, and a crown was placed on his head. He rode out to win many battles and gain the victory.

The Lamb of God now breaks the first seal on the scroll. A white horse appears with a rider going out to win battles and has a bow but no arrows. Is this significant? Some believe the rider on the white horse is Jesus Christ, but He is the Lamb who opened the seal. Seems more likely it is one who imitates the Lord Jesus, the antichrist. Likely he wins over the world by promising peace to the world and later reveals he is against Christ and not just instead of Christ.

REFLECT

What you are now reading is future. Whether or not you understand what is being presented, as a believer in Jesus you can be confident that you are safe in Him.

RESPOND

Sometimes believers see similar expressions and think they refer to the same thing—such as "white horse" in this passage. Teach others to pay careful attention to the surrounding passage and what is being said.

DAY 3

RECEIVE

Revelation 6:3-4

³ When the Lamb broke the second seal, I heard the second living being say, "Come!" ⁴ Then another horse appeared, a red one. Its rider was given a mighty sword and the authority to take peace from the earth. And there was war and slaughter everywhere.

Some Bible interpreters think all prophecy has been fulfilled in the past. The second seal reveals a time when peace is taken from the entire earth. It is not possible to fit this into any historical period that involves peace being taken from the entire earth. This is yet future. It is a period known as the 70th Week of Daniel (Daniel 9:27) and referred to by Jesus in Matthew 24.

REFLECT

Revelation gives you a glimpse into the future. It is not necessary that you understand all the details of what and how God will do things. Just know that He is in control and will eventually judge the earth for its rebellion against Him.

RESPOND

With your friend, think about the sovereignty of God from such passages as Proverbs 21:1 and 1 Timothy 6:15. See also the verse already seen in Revelation 1:8. The Bible has many other verses that stress God reigns over all—He is Almighty.

REVELATION

DAY 4

RECEIVE

Revelation 6:5-6

⁵ When the Lamb broke the third seal, I heard the third living being say, "Come!" I looked up and saw a black horse, and its rider was holding a pair of scales in his hand. ⁶ And I heard a voice from among the four living beings say, "A loaf of wheat bread or three loaves of barley will cost a day's pay. And don't waste the olive oil and wine."

After the red horse appeared and caused worldwide warfare, a black horse appears. The color is fitting because this will be a time of worldwide mourning and famine. A day's wages would only buy one loaf of wheat bread or three made of barley. A working man would not be able to feed his family. Not to "waste" the oil and wine seems best understood not to harm them. Seems the wealthy will have luxury items while others starve.

REFLECT

Think about government programs intended to help the poor. Often the poor are not significantly helped while the rich get richer. Revelation tells of such an extreme time coming.

RESPOND

In the first century the local church was instructed to take care of the poor. See 1 Timothy 5:9-10 for an example. What is your local church doing to help members in need? What are you doing personally to help?

WEEK 12: REVELATION 5, 6

DAY 5

RECEIVE

Revelation 6:7-8

⁷ When the Lamb broke the fourth seal, I heard the fourth living being say, "Come!" ⁸ I looked up and saw a horse whose color was pale green. Its rider was named Death, and his companion was the Grave. These two were given authority over one-fourth of the earth, to kill with the sword and famine and disease and wild animals.

The rider on the pale green horse is called "Death, and his companion was the Grave." The word underlying "Grave" is *hadēs*. At the time of physical death the body goes to the grave, but the spirit of the unbeliever goes to *hadēs*. (The spirit of the believer goes to be with Jesus.) Authority will be given over one-fourth of the earth to kill with famine, disease and wild animals. Nothing like this has ever taken place in history.

REFLECT

Think of what a terrible time for those living on earth at the time of these events. Regardless of what is seen now, nothing compares to this time in the future when God pours out judgments on earth.

RESPOND

With your friend, read Luke 16:19-31 that tells about an unbeliever being in *hadēs*. Notice he was told if others do not believe Moses and the prophets they would not believe even if someone rose from the dead. Read Revelation 20:11-15 to see that those in *hadēs* will someday be thrown into the lake of fire.

WEEK 13: REVELATION 6

RECEIVE

DAY 1

Revelation 6:9-10

⁹ When the Lamb broke the fifth seal, I saw under the altar the souls of all who had been martyred for the word of God and for being faithful in their testimony. ¹⁰ They shouted to the Lord and said, "O Sovereign Lord, holy and true, how long before you judge the people who belong to this world and avenge our blood for what they have done to us?"

This passage reveals the outcry of those who have died for their faith in Jesus. They had not lived during the Church age or they would have been resurrected as indicated in 1 Thessalonians 4:13-18. They had been killed earlier in the Tribulation. They cried out to God and wondered how long it would be before He brought judgment on those who had tortured and killed them.

REFLECT

Think of those who have given their lives for Jesus during your lifetime. Although perhaps not in your region, you surely have heard about such. Pray for their families.

RESPOND

As you think of sharing what you are learning with a friend, you may not be able to meet personally. In this age of digital technology, use it to contact and encourage others.

RECEIVE

DAY 2

Revelation 6:11

¹¹ Then a white robe was given to each of them. And they were told to rest a little longer until the full number of their brothers and sisters—their fellow servants of Jesus who were to be martyred—had joined them.

The martyrs crying out for justice are told to wait longer. There would be others who would die for their faith in Jesus. A white robe was given to these now crying out, representing the righteous acts of saints (see Revelation 19:8). There will be many martyred for their faith during the seven-year Tribulation, and they will join those already martyred.

REFLECT

Think how sad it is for people to lose their lives for the sake of Jesus. Consider also the rewards that will be waiting for them.

RESPOND

While thinking of the future in the passages in Revelation, remind people no one is really certain about tomorrow. Whether one dies from an accident, pandemic, or old age, someday everyone will be in eternity. Urge them to trust in Jesus as Savior before it is eternally too late. Remind them of what 2 Corinthians 6:2 says.

WEEK 13: REVELATION 6

DAY 3

RECEIVE

Revelation 6:12-14

¹² I watched as the Lamb broke the sixth seal, and there was a great earthquake. The sun became as dark as black cloth, and the moon became as red as blood. ¹³ Then the stars of the sky fell to the earth like green figs falling from a tree shaken by a strong wind. ¹⁴ The sky was rolled up like a scroll, and all of the mountains and islands were moved from their places.

There is an interesting contrast in this passage. The word the apostle used for "Lamb" referred to a little lamb, yet great eruptions in nature occur as the little lamb opens the sixth seal. The entire world will become aware that severe judgments are coming. Will this cause people to turn to Jesus? The answer is given in the following verses.

REFLECT

Think of the circumstances and people who helped you to see your need to place your trust in Jesus. Share your testimony with others.

RESPOND

As you talk with a friend about these events in Revelation, talk about how the sovereign God of the universe is in complete control of what occurs. See Colossians 1:15-17 that tells about Jesus holding all things together. He is in absolute control of what He created.

RECEIVE

DAY 4

Revelation 6:15-16

¹⁵ Then everyone—the kings of the earth, the rulers, the generals, the wealthy, the powerful, and every slave and free person—all hid themselves in the caves and among the rocks of the mountains. ¹⁶ And they cried to the mountains and the rocks, "Fall on us and hide us from the face of the one who sits on the throne and from the wrath of the Lamb."

When circumstances become extremely difficult, will they cause people to turn to Jesus? This passage reveals people would rather have the rocks and mountains crush them to death so they would not have to face the wrath of the Lamb. This also reveals the people do not realize they will still stand before God as their judge.

REFLECT

Do you know of any who think physical death will spare them from meeting God face to face? Far worse than physical death is spiritual death.

RESPOND

When the Bible speaks of death it often refers to spiritual death. Romans 6:23 has more than physical death in mind. Physical death is the separation of the soul from the body; spiritual death is the separation of the person from God for eternity.

WEEK 13: REVELATION 6

DAY 5

RECEIVE

Revelation 6:17

¹⁷ "For the great day of their wrath has come, and who is able to survive?"

Many people welcome talk about the love of God, but they do not want to hear about His wrath. They prefer sermons that emphasize the grace of God and omit any reference to sin and judgment. This setting in Revelation reveals there will come a time when the wrath of God will be poured out on a rebellious God-rejecting world.

REFLECT

Do you understand that although God is long-suffering and wants all to come to Jesus (see 2 Peter 3:9), there will be a time when judgment will come on those who do not (see Revelation 20:11-15)?

RESPOND

Believers in Jesus need to love what God loves and hate what He hates. See Proverbs 6:16-19 for seven things God hates. See also 2 Timothy 4:1-4 where the apostle Paul writes why the gospel should be urgently proclaimed now.

Week 14: Revelation 7

DAY 1

RECEIVE

Revelation 7:1-2

¹ Then I saw four angels standing at the four corners of the earth, holding back the four winds so they did not blow on the earth or the sea, or even on any tree. ² And I saw another angel coming up from the east, carrying the seal of the living God. And he shouted to those four angels, who had been given power to harm land and sea.

The winds of judgment are held back from the North, South, East and West. Revelation 6 had ended by saying, "And they cried to the mountains and the rocks, "Fall on us and hide us from the face of the one who sits on the throne and from the wrath of the Lamb. For the great day of their wrath has come, and who is able to survive?" (vv. 16-17). This indicates that the severest part of the Tribulation period is about to begin. Something is to be done before that.

REFLECT

Revelation 7 will answer who will be able to stand during the severest time of the Tribulation period.

RESPOND

Times may be difficult in some places now, but in the future tough times will envelope the entire universe. Be sure your trust is in the Lord Jesus.

DAY 2

RECEIVE

Revelation 7:3-8

³ "Wait! Don't harm the land or the sea or the trees until we have placed the seal of God on the foreheads of his servants." ⁴ And I heard how many were marked with the seal of God—144,000 were sealed from all the tribes of Israel: ⁵ from Judah 12,000, from Reuben 12,000, from Gad 12,000, ⁶ from Asher 12,000, from Naphtali 12,000, from Manasseh 12,000, ⁷ from Simeon 12,000, from Levi 12,000, from Issachar 12,000, ⁸ from Zebulun 12,000, from Joseph 12,000, from Benjamin 12,000.

The angel commanded the four angels to wait on pouring out judgment. Yet to be done was marking the 12 tribes of Israel with the seal of God, 12,000 from each tribe. These 144,000 would be marked by God in contrast to unbelievers who would receive the mark of the beast, seen in Revelation 13:16-17. Likely this would assure that these would live through the last half of the seven-year Tribulation in spite of the horrible judgments to come.

REFLECT

Marvel at God's plan to protect even in the midst of bringing judgment.

RESPOND

With a friend, read Matthew 24:21-22 that records the words of Jesus telling of the time in the future that will be worse than at any time before and will never be repeated after that.

WEEK 14: REVELATION 7

DAY 3

RECEIVE

Revelation 7:9-10

⁹ After this I saw a vast crowd, too great to count, from every nation and tribe and people and language, standing in front of the throne and before the Lamb. They were clothed in white robes and held palm branches in their hands. ¹⁰ And they were shouting with a great roar, "Salvation comes from our God who sits on the throne and from the Lamb!"

Because the believers during the Church age are caught up to meet Jesus in the air (see 1 Thessalonians 4:13-18), only living unbelievers are left to enter the Tribulation. Some wonder if anyone will be saved during the Tribulation. Revelation 7:4-8 tells of 144,000 Jewish people who will be saved, and verse 9 tells of Gentiles from "every nation and tribe and people and language" who will be saved.

REFLECT

Thank the Lord that He has some who will trust Him as Savior in every age of time. Salvation has always been by grace through faith in believing God's promises.

RESPOND

Some think there are different plans of salvation for different times. Even before the Mosaic law was given the Bible reveals in Genesis 15:6 that Abram (later known as Abraham), believed in God and he was counted as righteous because of his faith in God.

DAY 4

RECEIVE

Revelation 7:11-12

¹¹ And all the angels were standing around the throne and around the elders and the four living beings. And they fell before the throne with their faces to the ground and worshiped God. ¹² They sang, "Amen! Blessing and glory and wisdom and thanksgiving and honor and power and strength belong to our God forever and ever! Amen."

What a magnificent scene of those who bowed down to worship the Lord. Although various Bible versions say they "sang," the common word for "saying" was used. They were proclaiming the greatness and wonder of God and all that belongs to Him "forever and ever. Amen." This serves as an example of pleasing God by our worship.

REFLECT

Think of various ways you can thank God for His worthiness, which is worshiping Him.

RESPOND

Talk with a friend about the various ways used to worship God. Which seems the most important to each of you?

WEEK 14: REVELATION 7

DAY 5

RECEIVE

Revelation 7:13-14

¹³ Then one of the twenty-four elders asked me, "Who are these who are clothed in white? Where did they come from?" ¹⁴ And I said to him, "Sir, you are the one who knows." Then he said to me, "These are the ones who died in the great tribulation. They have washed their robes in the blood of the Lamb and made them white."

The apostle John was asked a question he did not know how to answer. He realized that the one who asked the question knew the answer so he asked him. The answer came that these were ones who were martyred during the great tribulation. It is a scene at the end of the seven years of Tribulation looking back over those who had been killed for their faith during this time.

REFLECT

It is wonderful that those who have given their lives for Jesus will be rewarded someday. The people in this passage had given the ultimate sacrifice for the Lord Jesus who sacrificed all for them.

RESPOND

Encourage others with the words of Jesus, "I am the resurrection and the life. Anyone who believes in me will live, even after dying." Those martyred during the Tribulation would benefit from that promise. Even people today can have that same assurance when a loved one dies who has believed in Jesus for salvation.

Week 15: Revelation 7, 8

DAY 1

RECEIVE

Revelation 7:15

¹⁵ "That is why they stand in front of God's throne and serve him day and night in his Temple. And he who sits on the throne will give them shelter."

One of the 24 elders continued to tell the apostle John about those who had been martyred during the Tribulation and were now praising God before the throne. They serve God "day and night in his temple." They are also promised that God "who sits on the throne will give them shelter." What does this shelter include? More is explained in the following verses.

REFLECT

Thank the Lord that even though circumstances may be extreme, God is your ultimate protector.

RESPOND

The Ascent Psalms (120-134) promised God's care for those marching up to Jerusalem to celebrate the feasts. These psalms have been of encouragement to believers over the years. Suggest to a friend that these be read for a reminder of how God cares for His people. Possibly follow a plan to read one of these psalms each day. Even more protection will be provided in eternity.

DAY 2

RECEIVE

Revelation 7:16-17

[16] "They will never again be hungry or thirsty; they will never be scorched by the heat of the sun. [17] For the Lamb on the throne will be their Shepherd. He will lead them to springs of life-giving water. And God will wipe every tear from their eyes."

Those martyred for their faith during the Tribulation are promised they will never go through such horrible times again. Above all, "God will wipe every tear from their eyes." One can only imagine the heartache and tears shed when these were martyred, but never again will that occur because God will wipe all tears from their eyes.

REFLECT

It is one thing to stand for Christ when friends do not appreciate your opinions, but think of the grief of those families and loved ones who had someone put to death because of believing in Jesus.

RESPOND

Read Revelation 21:3-4 to see that when all believers are with God in the New Jerusalem all the sorrows of their previous lives will be gone forever.

WEEK 15: REVELATION 7, 8

DAY 3

RECEIVE

Revelation 8:1-2

¹ When the Lamb broke the seventh seal on the scroll, there was silence throughout heaven for about half an hour. ² I saw the seven angels who stand before God, and they were given seven trumpets.

After the brief interlude after the sixth seal was broken, the seventh seal is broken. The judgments on earth will become more severe. The seventh seal introduces seven trumpets and each of them will describe judgments on earth. Perhaps the silence for about a half hour was because of the terrible judgments expected. The seven angels are now given seven trumpets, the contents of which will be revealed in the following verses.

REFLECT

Rejoice that if you have placed your faith in Jesus as Savior, you will not experience these judgments in the Tribulation. There will be troubles on earth, but nothing in comparison to those that will occur during the 70th Week of Daniel, known as the Tribulation.

RESPOND

To distinguish the troubles of this time in contrast to the time in the Great Tribulation, see John 16:33 for the troubles in these times, and Matthew 24:21-22 that refers to the Tribulation of the future.

DAY 4

RECEIVE

Revelation 8:3

³ Then another angel with a gold incense burner came and stood at the altar. And a great amount of incense was given to him to mix with the prayers of God's people as an offering on the gold altar before the throne.

Again it is seen that incense is associated with prayers. It should be encouraging to believers of all times to realize their prayers are sweet incense to God. In this case, the prayers were mixed with the incense as an "offering on the gold altar before the throne." In the Old Testament many offerings were presented and sacrificed. Even today believers can present offerings pleasing to God.

REFLECT

What can you offer to God today as an offering? Your prayers are pleasing to Him, but you can also present your life as a pleasing sacrifice.

RESPOND

With a friend, read Romans 12:1-2 that will show the kind of sacrifice believers can give today that will please God and be an act of worship.

WEEK 15: REVELATION 7, 8

DAY 5

RECEIVE

Revelation 8:4-5

⁴ The smoke of the incense, mixed with the prayers of God's holy people, ascended up to God from the altar where the angel had poured them out. ⁵ Then the angel filled the incense burner with fire from the altar and threw it down upon the earth; and thunder crashed, lightning flashed, and there was a terrible earthquake.

These verses reveal what the angel did after the prayers with the incense went up to God. The incense burner was filled with fire and thrown to the earth. There have been violent storms in the past, but what happens to the earth now will be greater and more extensive than anything seen before. This leads into what the seven angels will do with the seven trumpets.

REFLECT

God has warned those on earth before with events from nature. Have people turned to God as a result? Some do; many do not. Even after people think about God during a major incident, many neglect Him afterwards.

RESPOND

Pray that whatever difficulty you may be going through now you will learn from it and remain with a tender heart towards God afterwards. It is seen in Revelation 6:15-17 that after warnings of severe judgment came through nature, people turned away from God, not to Him.

RECEIVE

DAY 1

Revelation 8:6-7

⁶ Then the seven angels with the seven trumpets prepared to blow their mighty blasts. ⁷ The first angel blew his trumpet, and hail and fire mixed with blood were thrown down on the earth. One-third of the earth was set on fire, one-third of the trees were burned, and all the green grass was burned.

There is no reason to assume this language is symbolic and means something it does not say. The plagues in Egypt were real before the Passover in Exodus 12 and these judgments on rebellious mankind will also be real. In Exodus only Egypt was affected (with the exception of the Israelites at times); here the entire earth is affected. Those who think all prophecy was fulfilled in the past must make these judgments symbolic to mean something they do not say.

REFLECT

In your Bible study do not be quick to make things mean something they do not say. Some language is symbolic but do not force Scripture to mean something entirely different than what is expressed.

RESPOND

Talk with a friend about how horrible it will be to be living at the time described in Revelation 8. God's wrath is being poured out on an unbelieving world.

Day 2

RECEIVE

Revelation 8:8-9

⁸ Then the second angel blew his trumpet, and a great mountain of fire was thrown into the sea. One-third of the water in the sea became blood, ⁹ one-third of all things living in the sea died, and one-third of all the ships on the sea were destroyed.

Massive judgments and catastrophes continue. Notice the repetition of thirds in these judgments. The devastation will be massive. Lives and livelihoods will be destroyed. It's impossible to comprehend the devastation these judgments will cause. It is not necessary to understand all of it, but to believe it.

REFLECT

It would be a terrible thing to be living at the time of the Great Tribulation on earth. Pray for friends to trust Jesus as Savior now so they will not need to go through that time.

RESPOND

Remind a friend that the need is not to understand everything in the Bible, but to believe what is written. When thinking of these incredible events on earth, thank the Lord that those who believe in Him now will not need to experience them.

WEEK 16: REVELATION 8

DAY 3

RECEIVE

Revelation 8:10-11

¹⁰ Then the third angel blew his trumpet, and a great star fell from the sky, burning like a torch. It fell on one-third of the rivers and on the springs of water. 11 The name of the star was Bitterness. It made one-third of the water bitter, and many people died from drinking the bitter water.

How could a great star cause all of this damage? God used a star for blessing when He guided the wise men to Jerusalem at the time of Jesus' birth. Then He used the same star to guide them to the house where little Jesus was living (see Matthew 2). Here in Revelation, God is using a star to bring judgment, not announcing blessing.

REFLECT

Remember that God is in control of the universe. He is able to use it as He wishes.

RESPOND

Read Hebrews 1:1-3 and Colossians 1:15-17 to see that the Son of God holds all things together. He is in ultimate control and can use the universe for blessing or judgment.

DAY 4

RECEIVE

Revelation 8:12

¹² Then the fourth angel blew his trumpet, and one-third of the sun was struck, and one-third of the moon, and one-third of the stars, and they became dark. And one-third of the day was dark, and also one-third of the night.

God created lights in the sky to light the earth (see Genesis 1:14-18). He had brought darkness in Egypt when Pharaoh refused to let His people go (see Exodus 10:21-23). In Revelation, God brings judgment that reduces the light on earth. The judgments seem to be getting more and more severe, but more is yet to come.

REFLECT

Are you more impressed now that God has created the universe and is able to use it in ways that He desires?

RESPOND

Join with someone in thanking God that in the great universe He looked down on mankind and sent His Son to be the Savior of the world.

DAY 5

RECEIVE

Revelation 8:13

> ¹³ Then I looked, and I heard a single eagle crying loudly as it flew through the air, "Terror, terror, terror to all who belong to this world because of what will happen when the last three angels blow their trumpets."

As terrible as the judgments have been as revealed by the four angels with trumpets, now an eagle announces the last three will be worse. The words "Terror, terror, terror" are translated by some as "Woe, woe, woe." The coming judgments will be worse than the first four as God brings judgment on the world.

REFLECT

Think some more about the fact that God is not only a God of love, as demonstrated by sending His Son to die for us, but He is also a God of holiness and justice. Some want only to hear about His love, but that is only one aspect of our glorious God.

RESPOND

Do you know of a Bible passage that tells you people primarily want to hear only the good things about God? Read 2 Timothy 4:1-4 that tells how important it is to proclaim the gospel now while people may still listen.

Week 17: Revelation 9

DAY 1

RECEIVE

Revelation 9:1–2

¹ Then the fifth angel blew his trumpet, and I saw a star that had fallen to earth from the sky, and he was given the key to the shaft of the bottomless pit. ² When he opened it, smoke poured out as though from a huge furnace, and the sunlight and air turned dark from the smoke.

The first of the three terrors, or woes, are now poured out on the earth. The "bottomless pit" or "abyss" was likely inhabited by demons (see Luke 8:31). When it was opened, smoke poured from it and darkened the sun and turned the air dark. There is no need to try to use natural phenomena to explain this. God is at work in bringing judgment on the earth.

REFLECT

Those who love Jesus know God as one who frees from all condemnation, but someday God's judgment will fall on unbelievers.

RESPOND

With a friend, read passages such as John 3:18; 5:24; and Romans 8:1. May you rejoice in knowing there is no judgment or condemnation for the person who is in Christ Jesus.

REVELATION

DAY 2

RECEIVE

Revelation 9:3-4

³ Then locusts came from the smoke and descended on the earth, and they were given power to sting like scorpions. ⁴ They were told not to harm the grass or plants or trees, but only the people who did not have the seal of God on their foreheads.

From the thick smoke came locusts who had power to sting like scorpions. These likely were demons who looked to the apostle John like locusts. They were instructed not to harm vegetation but only those who did not have the seal of God on their foreheads. This is a judgment on unbelievers—those who had rejected Jesus Christ as Savior.

REFLECT

Notice that even during the Great Tribulation those who turn to God in faith are protected.

RESPOND

Read Revelation 7:1-4 to see who had received the "seal of God." These were being protected from being tormented or dying in the Tribulation.

WEEK 17: REVELATION 9

DAY 3

RECEIVE

Revelation 9:5-6

⁵ They were told not to kill them but to torture them for five months with pain like the pain of a scorpion sting. ⁶ In those days people will seek death but will not find it. They will long to die, but death will flee from them!

The demons were told to torment those who had not received the seal of God on their foreheads. They were to torment them for five months. The pain will be so excruciating that unbelievers will want to die but be unable to do so. The world may talk now of those who commit suicide but even that would not be possible during the Tribulation.

REFLECT

There are few things sadder than a loved one who has committed suicide. During the Tribulation unbelievers will suffer such pain they will want to die but be unable to do so.

RESPOND

Do all you can to encourage others in despair not to take their lives. Believing in God can give them hope. How sad it will be in the Tribulation for unbelievers to be in such pain they will want to die but not be able.

REVELATION

DAY 4

RECEIVE

Revelation 9:7-10

⁷ The locusts looked like horses prepared for battle. They had what looked like gold crowns on their heads, and their faces looked like human faces. ⁸ They had hair like women's hair and teeth like the teeth of a lion. ⁹ They wore armor made of iron, and their wings roared like an army of chariots rushing into battle. ¹⁰ They had tails that stung like scorpions, and for five months they had the power to torment people.

Remember that the apostle John is writing in the first century and trying to describe what these things looked like to him. These creatures John was describing would torment unbelievers for five months. Only those who had the seal of God on their foreheads would be exempt from this torment and suffering.

REFLECT

Marvel again how God protects His own. In the Tribulation, those around them would be in torment and wanting to die while the believers were protected.

RESPOND

Do not be too hard on the apostle John for using so many symbolic descriptions. Imagine what you would have written in his situation.

RECEIVE

DAY 5

Revelation 9:11-12

¹¹ Their king is the angel from the bottomless pit; his name in Hebrew is Abaddon, and in Greek, Apollyon—the Destroyer. ¹² The first terror is past, but look, two more terrors are coming!

Verse 11 gives us a clue the bottomless pit is inhabited by demons. Their leader is known as the destroyer and that is certainly what he and his subordinates are doing in the Tribulation. The hordes of demons are released to torture unbelievers for five months. Verse 12 indicates the first terror, or woe, is passed but there are still two more to come.

REFLECT

There is only one devil, also known as Satan, but there are many demons who serve as his emissaries. For the believer today, there is the assurance that greater is He who is in you (the Holy Spirit), than he who is in the world (see 1 John 4:4).

RESPOND

With a friend, read the attacks of the devil on Jesus in Matthew 4:1-11. Jesus was tempted, in the sense that He was "tested." Because He was wholly God as well as wholly man, there was nothing in Him that made Him even think about yielding to the testing of the devil.

Week 18: Revelation 9, 10

RECEIVE

DAY 1

Revelation 9:13-16

[13] Then the sixth angel blew his trumpet, and I heard a voice speaking from the four horns of the gold altar that stands in the presence of God. [14] And the voice said to the sixth angel who held the trumpet, "Release the four angels who are bound at the great Euphrates River." [15] Then the four angels who had been prepared for this hour and day and month and year were turned loose to kill one-third of all the people on earth. [16] I heard the size of their army, which was 200 million mounted troops.

The angels who were released must have been fallen angels who are demons. There would be no reason for unfallen angels to be bound. They were prepared for this specific time to kill a third of all the people on earth. Earlier a fourth had been killed (see Revelation 6:7-8), so this is a third of those remaining. They were accompanied by an army of 200 million mounted troops. They would be coming across the Euphrates River.

REFLECT

Think how horrible these judgments will be during the Great Tribulation. The Church, the Bride of Christ, will not be on earth at that time. It has been promised to be saved even from the time of this trouble that would come on the entire world (see Revelation 3:10).

RESPOND

Give thanks to the Lord that present-day believers in Jesus will not be on earth during this time. Pray for others to trust in Jesus as Savior so they will not be here then.

REVELATION

DAY 2

RECEIVE

Revelation 9:17-19

¹⁷ And in my vision, I saw the horses and the riders sitting on them. The riders wore armor that was fiery red and dark blue and yellow. The horses had heads like lions, and fire and smoke and burning sulfur billowed from their mouths. ¹⁸ One-third of all the people on earth were killed by these three plagues—by the fire and smoke and burning sulfur that came from the mouths of the horses. ¹⁹ Their power was in their mouths and in their tails. For their tails had heads like snakes, with the power to injure people.

This passage describes the horses of the 200 million mounted troops. In Bible times, the horse was a military animal. Here the horses are seen as doing the destruction, which leads some to think that the horses in this passage are really demons. Whoever they are, the plague of fire, smoke and brimstone will kill a third of the remaining people on earth. They also had the power to injure as well as kill.

REFLECT

Do not be discouraged by what you don't understand in the book of Revelation. The apostle John is describing what he saw in a vision. The description by someone else might be different but the results would be the same.

RESPOND

Thank the Lord that even though there are many things in the Bible you do not understand, there is enough you understand to give you confidence in His sovereign control. God holds all things together, as seen in Colossians 1:15-17. Read these verses to see what they say about the Lord Jesus Christ.

WEEK 18: REVELATION 9, 10

DAY 3

RECEIVE

Revelation 9:20-21

²⁰ But the people who did not die in these plagues still refused to repent of their evil deeds and turn to God. They continued to worship demons and idols made of gold, silver, bronze, stone, and wood—idols that can neither see nor hear nor walk! ²¹ And they did not repent of their murders or their witchcraft or their sexual immorality or their thefts.

Sometimes it is thought that if a person experiences difficulty it will cause the individual to turn to God. Not so during the Tribulation period. The more difficulty experienced, the more they turned away from the true God to false gods. The word translated "witchcraft" is the one from which the word "pharmacy" is derived. Some translations render it as "sorceries." It has to do with drugs. During the Tribulation the drug culture will be worse than ever, as well as sexual immorality and thievery.

REFLECT

Does this Scripture passage help you to see that difficulties do not always cause a person to turn to God? As has been said, "The sun melts the ice but hardens the clay." Difficulties only bring out what is in a person's heart.

RESPOND

Read Revelation 16:8-9 to see that as these horrible times continued to come on people, they still did not repent and turn to God.

REVELATION

DAY 4

RECEIVE

Revelation 10:1–3

¹ Then I saw another mighty angel coming down from heaven, surrounded by a cloud, with a rainbow over his head. His face shone like the sun, and his feet were like pillars of fire. ² And in his hand was a small scroll that had been opened. He stood with his right foot on the sea and his left foot on the land. ³ And he gave a great shout like the roar of a lion. And when he shouted, the seven thunders answered.

In his vision, the apostle John sees a mighty angel coming down from heaven. It has a rainbow over its head. The rainbow was the symbol God used to promise there would never again be a worldwide flood. By standing with his feet on the land and the sea is an indication of power over the entire earth. To hear one giant thunder would have been significant, but John hears seven thunders answering the mighty angel who gave a great shout.

REFLECT

Think of John's difficulty trying to explain the vision he saw of the mighty angel. Do you wonder what the seven thunders said?

RESPOND

To see God's promise never to send another worldwide flood and for the rainbow to remind humanity of His promise, read Genesis 9:12–17. This also reminds readers the Genesis flood was a universal one and not a local flood because there have been many local floods since then.

WEEK 18: REVELATION 9, 10

DAY 5

RECEIVE

Revelation 10:4

⁴ When the seven thunders spoke, I was about to write. But I heard a voice from heaven saying, "Keep secret what the seven thunders said, and do not write it down."

Apparently the apostle John was impressed with what the seven thunders answered the mighty angels and was about to write what they said. He was instructed, however, to keep it a secret and not to write what he heard. It seems to be the curiosity of most people to want to know what they are not able to know. The book of Daniel has many prophecies, but at the conclusion God told him to seal up the book until the time of the end (see Daniel 12:3-4).

REFLECT

How is it with you? The Bible has told us many things clear to be understood. Do you spend more time thinking about that or questioning what the Bible does not tell us?

RESPOND

Human nature is seen in the first two human beings the Lord created—Adam and Eve. In the beautiful Garden of Eden they could eat of all the trees except one. Which do you think they wanted? Read Genesis 2:15-17 and Genesis 3:6-7 for the answer. Adam's sin poisoned the entire human race because everyone born afterwards inherited his sin nature, as Romans 5:12 says.

Week 19: Revelation 10, 11

RECEIVE

DAY 1

Revelation 10:5-7

⁵ Then the angel I saw standing on the sea and on the land raised his right hand toward heaven. ⁶ He swore an oath in the name of the one who lives forever and ever, who created the heavens and everything in them, the earth and everything in it, and the sea and everything in it. He said, "There will be no more delay. ⁷ When the seventh angel blows his trumpet, God's mysterious plan will be fulfilled. It will happen just as he announced it to his servants the prophets."

This angel swore an oath by the one "who created the heavens and everything in them." This answers the evolutionists about how these things came into being. The announcement that there would be "no more delay" has to do when the "seventh angel blows his trumpet." This does not occur until Revelation 16. There are many questions people would like to ask God. At this time His "mysterious plan will be fulfilled." God's program of the ages will be fully known then.

REFLECT

Do you have several questions you would like to ask God? Many people do. Perhaps when you are face to face with Jesus you will not be in need of more answers.

RESPOND

To get a glimpse of when the seventh angel blows his trumpet, read Revelation 16:17-18. Even though it is not known what all will take place in God's mysterious plan, Christ followers can have confidence in Him.

DAY 2

RECEIVE

Revelation 10:8-9

> ⁸ Then the voice from heaven spoke to me again: "Go and take the open scroll from the hand of the angel who is standing on the sea and on the land." ⁹ So I went to the angel and told him to give me the small scroll. "Yes, take it and eat it," he said. "It will be sweet as honey in your mouth, but it will turn sour in your stomach!"

This is not the only reference to the eating of a scroll. The Old Testament prophet Ezekiel was told to eat a scroll and announce coming judgment to God's people who were not honoring Him (see Ezekiel 3). This had to do with assimilating God's message. It seems the same is true when Jesus told the disciples to eat His body and drink His blood (see John 6:53-55). He was not suggesting cannibalism but believing in Him as Savior. To the apostle John in Revelation 10, the message would seem sweet at first but would turn sour as he better understood it.

REFLECT

Think about the times when you have read a book and really absorbed its contents. In that sense you "ate the book."

RESPOND

Read Leviticus 17:10-12 and Acts 15:19-21 to see both the Old Testament and New Testament prohibition about not eating or drinking blood. This would relate to both before and after Jesus instructed the disciples to eat His blood. The disciples would have been horrified if they thought Jesus was really telling them to eat His blood.

DAY 3

RECEIVE

Revelation 10:10-11

¹⁰ So I took the small scroll from the hand of the angel, and I ate it! It was sweet in my mouth, but when I swallowed it, it turned sour in my stomach. ¹¹ Then I was told, "You must prophesy again about many peoples, nations, languages, and kings."

God's message is sweet as people learn about Jesus shedding His blood for their sins. It becomes bitter, however, when one realizes the judgment that will fall on those who do not trust in Him as Savior. The instructions to John to "prophesy again" relates to the remainder of the book of Revelation as it predicts what will happen to "many peoples, nations, languages, and kings."

REFLECT

Have you also found the Scriptures to be of comfort as you learn about what Jesus has done for you? Do you become sad when you realize some of your loved ones have not trusted in Jesus as Savior?

RESPOND

Pray with a follower of Jesus. Thank God for all that has been provided for your salvation. Pray for loved ones and friends who have not yet trusted in Him as Savior.

DAY 4

RECEIVE

Revelation 11:1-3

¹ Then I was given a measuring stick, and I was told, "Go and measure the Temple of God and the altar, and count the number of worshipers. ² But do not measure the outer courtyard, for it has been turned over to the nations. They will trample the holy city for 42 months. ³ And I will give power to my two witnesses, and they will be clothed in burlap and will prophesy during those 1,260 days."

In measuring the temple, John was to leave out the outer courtyard where Gentiles were allowed to gather. What is known as the Times of the Gentiles was not to end yet. This time period began when the Babylonians gained control over Israel and continues until the second advent of Christ when He returns to earth at the end of the Tribulation. Two witnesses appear in burlap, the dress of mourning, and give predictions during three and a half years.

REFLECT

As the Tribulation continues in the future, there will be much mourning about the judgment of God that is about to fall. God is holy and just, and cannot allow sin to go unpunished.

RESPOND

Read Luke 21:20-24 to see what it will be like in the Tribulation before Jesus returns to earth. No believers of the present Church age will be present then, but there will be some who will turn to God during the Tribulation. Most will die for their faith.

WEEK 19: REVELATION 10, 11

DAY 5

RECEIVE

Revelation 11:4-6

⁴ These two prophets are the two olive trees and the two lampstands that stand before the Lord of all the earth. ⁵ If anyone tries to harm them, fire flashes from their mouths and consumes their enemies. This is how anyone who tries to harm them must die. ⁶ They have power to shut the sky so that no rain will fall for as long as they prophesy. And they have the power to turn the rivers and oceans into blood, and to strike the earth with every kind of plague as often as they wish.

There has been much speculation about the identity of the two prophets. Their powerful acts have similarities to other prophets, but similarities are not the same as identity. The Bible does not say who they are, which indicates that what they do is more important than who they are. They have powers given to them by God to consume their enemies and to turn rivers and oceans into blood. They will also bring plagues on the earth.

REFLECT

Think how scary it would be to be living at this future time in history. Some can escape God's judgment for a while, but it will eventually fall on them if they do not turn to Him by faith.

RESPOND

Join with a fellow Christian and talk about how precious it is to know Jesus as Savior who took your judgment for you. Think also on Hebrews 10:30-31 that tells how terrible it will be to undergo the judgment of God for those who keep rejecting Him.

RECEIVE

DAY 1

Revelation 11:7-8

⁷ When they complete their testimony, the beast that comes up out of the bottomless pit will declare war against them, and he will conquer them and kill them. ⁸ And their bodies will lie in the main street of Jerusalem, the city that is figuratively called "Sodom" and "Egypt," the city where their Lord was crucified.

This passage refers to the two witnesses, or prophets, who appear with great power on earth. The reference to "the" beast rather than "a" beast seems to refer to the beast of Revelation 13, known as the Antichrist. He is able to kill the two witnesses and their bodies "lie in the main street of Jerusalem." Because of its corruption, the city is likened to Sodom and Egypt in the Old Testament. The city is identified as the place where the Lord Jesus was crucified, which makes it clear it refers to Jerusalem.

REFLECT

Think how sad it will be for any believers in the area to have the two witnesses killed. Their deaths could not have occurred, however, without God allowing it.

RESPOND

Read Genesis 19:1-10 to see what the Bible says about Sodom. It is from this event that the word "sodomy" is derived.

REVELATION

DAY 2

RECEIVE

Revelation 11:9-10

⁹ And for three and a half days, all peoples, tribes, languages, and nations will stare at their bodies. No one will be allowed to bury them. ¹⁰ All the people who belong to this world will gloat over them and give presents to each other to celebrate the death of the two prophets who had tormented them.

The dead bodies of the two witnesses lie in the street for three and a half days and no one was allowed to bury them. Others of the world viewing their bodies have caused some to say this could not have happened until modern technology was invented. Such a view, however, limits what a miracle-working God is able to do. This is a time of celebration for unbelievers. To them it is like Christmas with the sharing of gifts because these witnesses were killed.

REFLECT

Have you observed times when unbelievers rejoiced about something tragic happening to believers? Do you rejoice with those who rejoice and weep with those who weep?

RESPOND

With a fellow believer, read Romans 12:14-16 and ask yourselves if you are doing what this passage instructs.

WEEK 20: REVELATION 11

DAY 3

RECEIVE

Revelation 11:11-13

¹¹ But after three and a half days, God breathed life into them, and they stood up! Terror struck all who were staring at them. ¹² Then a loud voice from heaven called to the two prophets, "Come up here!" And they rose to heaven in a cloud as their enemies watched. ¹³ At the same time there was a terrible earthquake that destroyed a tenth of the city. Seven thousand people died in that earthquake, and everyone else was terrified and gave glory to the God of heaven.

Imagine how frightening it was to those who were rejoicing over the death of the two witnesses to see them come back to life. Before this, the witnesses had supernatural power in overcoming their enemies. What might they do now? Instead of conquering more enemies, the two of them were caught up to heaven while being watched by their enemies. This was accompanied by an earthquake that destroyed a tenth of the city of Jerusalem causing 7000 people to die. This brought further terror to the survivors. They realized this was because of the power of God, but there is no indication they trusted in Jesus as Savior.

REFLECT

Can you imagine such devastation as John saw in his vision? Had you been a survivor of this, do you think you would have turned to God or away from Him?

RESPOND

Let this remind you of the need to pray for those who may be going through trials now. Pray that in the midst of the trials they will turn to God instead of away from Him.

RECEIVE — DAY 4

Revelation 11:14-15

¹⁴ The second terror is past, but look, the third terror is coming quickly. ¹⁵ Then the seventh angel blew his trumpet, and there were loud voices shouting in heaven: "The world has now become the Kingdom of our Lord and of his Christ, and he will reign forever and ever."

This passage introduces the announcement of the soon return of Jesus to the earth, known as the Second Advent. The First Advent was when He was born of the virgin Mary in Bethlehem. Down through history, there have been many earthly kingdoms, but now in John's vision the kingdom of the Lord Jesus Christ is about to be established on earth and He will reign forever and ever.

REFLECT

Think of the rejoicing there will be when the announcement is made that the kingdom of God will come to the earth and that Jesus will reign forever. He rules now in the lives of believers but then He will rule as the King of His kingdom on earth.

RESPOND

Examine your life and think of whether Jesus is ruling as Lord in your life now. To say that He is Lord is the same as saying He is God. As God, He should have full control of every believer's life. For His kingdom to come on earth is what is prayed for in Matthew 6:10.

WEEK 20: REVELATION 11

DAY 5

RECEIVE

Revelation 11:16-18

¹⁶ The twenty-four elders sitting on their thrones before God fell with their faces to the ground and worshiped him. ¹⁷ And they said, "We give thanks to you, Lord God, the Almighty, the one who is and who always was, for now you have assumed your great power and have begun to reign. ¹⁸ The nations were filled with wrath, but now the time of your wrath has come. It is time to judge the dead and reward your servants the prophets, as well as your holy people, and all who fear your name, from the least to the greatest. It is time to destroy all who have caused destruction on the earth."

The twenty-four elders are mentioned various times in the book of Revelation. Here they are seen flat on their faces worshiping God. They gave thanks to God for who He is and acknowledged He was about to begin reigning on the earth. They also recognized it was time for God to judge the dead and reward believers who feared God's name. Many believers had died for their faith. Here the twenty-four elders say it is "time to destroy all who have caused destruction on the earth."

REFLECT

Consider that God is holy and cannot approve evil of any kind. Even though it seems He has delayed His judgment at the present time, there will come a time when His judgment will be meted out.

RESPOND

Talk with a fellow believer about serving a God who is both holy and just. Were it not for the sacrifice of Christ on the cross no one could escape His judgment. For those who trust in Jesus, however, the righteousness of Christ is placed on their account. For those who do not trust in Jesus, they will have to pay for their own sins, as Romans 6:23 says.

Week 21: Revelation 11, 12

RECEIVE

DAY 1

Revelation 11:19

[19] Then, in heaven, the Temple of God was opened and the Ark of his covenant could be seen inside the Temple. Lightning flashed, thunder crashed and roared, and there was an earthquake and a terrible hailstorm.

The apostle John now saw in his vision the temple of God in heaven with the ark of the covenant inside of it. Both the temple and ark related to the nation Israel. The Church does not have a physical building known as the temple on earth or in heaven. The lightning, thunder, earthquake and hailstorm will again be seen in Revelation 16 as the bowl judgments are poured out.

REFLECT

Do you see that terrible judgments of nature will come on the earth at the end of the Tribulation period? God controls nature and these could not have occurred apart from Him.

RESPOND

For an example of the temple of God during the Church age, read 2 Corinthians 6:14-16. Although He is everywhere present, God Himself indwells believers.

REVELATION

RECEIVE

DAY 2

Revelation 12:1-2

¹ Then I witnessed in heaven an event of great significance. I saw a woman clothed with the sun, with the moon beneath her feet, and a crown of twelve stars on her head. ² She was pregnant, and she cried out because of her labor pains and the agony of giving birth.

There has been much debate about the identity of the woman in Revelation 12. She is symbolic because no woman has undergone what this woman has. It seems best to consider this a picture of Israel who gave physical birth to the Messiah, the Savior of the world. Israel suffered greatly before the Messiah was born and has suffered greatly since that time because of antisemitism. Even some church groups are opposed to the nation of Israel, through which Jesus was born into the world.

REFLECT

What is your attitude toward the nation of Israel and the Jewish people? In John 4:22 Jesus told the Samaritan woman, "salvation comes through the Jews."

RESPOND

Consider what the Bible says about Abraham and his descendants, the Jewish people. Read passages such as Genesis 12:1-3; 17:18-20; and Romans 9:1-5.

WEEK 21: REVELATION 11, 12

DAY 3

RECEIVE

Revelation 12:3-4

³ Then I witnessed in heaven another significant event. I saw a large red dragon with seven heads and ten horns, with seven crowns on his heads. ⁴ His tail swept away one-third of the stars in the sky, and he threw them to the earth. He stood in front of the woman as she was about to give birth, ready to devour her baby as soon as it was born.

As this passage reveals later, the dragon is Satan. When Jesus was a baby, Satan used King Herod to try to snuff out His life (see Matthew 2:16). It seems this outburst of Satan's wrath will occur in the middle of the seven-year Tribulation, for Satan will use the revived Roman Empire to inflict judgment on the world. At this time his man will seat himself in the temple of God and demand to be worshiped. This will be the abomination of desolation spoken of by Daniel the prophet, and by Paul in 2 Thessalonians.

REFLECT

Think how horrible it will be for those on earth during the last half of the Tribulation. Thank the Lord for salvation that will keep you from this time.

RESPOND

To check out references to the "abomination of desolation," read Daniel 9:27 and 2 Thessalonians 2:1-4. Satan has always wanted to be worshiped instead of the Lord Jesus Christ, and he will put his representative (the Antichrist) in the temple to be worshiped during the Tribulation.

DAY 4

RECEIVE

Revelation 12:5-6

⁵ She gave birth to a son who was to rule all nations with an iron rod. And her child was snatched away from the dragon and was caught up to God and to his throne. ⁶ And the woman fled into the wilderness, where God had prepared a place to care for her for 1,260 days.

Only the Lord Jesus Christ qualifies as one who will "rule all nations with an iron rod" (see Psalm 2:8-9). Being caught up to God seems to refer to the ascension of Jesus, recorded in Acts 1:9. The woman (Israel) being protected for 1260 days is a time period of three and a half years of 30-day months, which was the measurement of months in Bible times.

REFLECT

Even in times of persecution God will protect a remnant of believers. Thank the Lord for His grace.

RESPOND

Look ahead to Revelation 19:15-16 to see that when Jesus returns to earth at the end of the Tribulation He will rule the nations with a rod of iron.

DAY 5

RECEIVE

Revelation 12:7-9

⁷ Then there was war in heaven. Michael and his angels fought against the dragon and his angels. ⁸ And the dragon lost the battle, and he and his angels were forced out of heaven. ⁹ This great dragon—the ancient serpent called the devil, or Satan, the one deceiving the whole world—was thrown down to the earth with all his angels.

This passage clearly identifies the dragon as the "devil, or Satan." Michael and his angels were stronger than Satan and his angels. Satan's angels are fallen angels who are demons to carry out his will. Note that Satan is described as one "deceiving the whole world." In the temptation of Jesus, Satan offered Him the kingdoms of the world if Jesus would bow down and worship him. Jesus did not say Satan did not have these to give.

REFLECT

You can be thankful that the one who indwells you is greater than he who is in the world, as the Bible says in 1 John 4:4.

RESPOND

Talk to a fellow believer about the temptation Jesus faced, as recorded in Matthew 4:8-10, when Satan offered Him the kingdoms of the world if He would bow down and worship him.

Week 22: Revelation 12, 13

RECEIVE

DAY 1

Revelation 12:10

¹⁰ Then I heard a loud voice shouting across the heavens, "It has come at last— salvation and power and the Kingdom of our God, and the authority of his Christ. For the accuser of our brothers and sisters has been thrown down to earth—the one who accuses them before our God day and night."

These verses reveal a climax is coming as a heavenly voice makes it known. This anticipates the 1000-year rule of Christ on earth. In this passage another name, or description, of Satan is seen. He is called "the accuser of our brothers and sisters." Note that the devil "accuses them before our God day and night." There are examples of this in the Scripture and none is more graphic than what happened to Job in the first two chapters of the book named after him.

REFLECT

Think about the comfort in the fact that Satan can never go beyond what God allows.

RESPOND

Take time with a believer in Christ to scan the first two chapters of the book of Job. Especially notice the following verses: 1:8-12 and 2:4-7. Talk about how comforting it is that God sets limits on what Satan can do.

REVELATION

RECEIVE

DAY 2

Revelation 12:11-12

[11] "And they have defeated him by the blood of the Lamb and by their testimony. And they did not love their lives so much that they were afraid to die. [12] Therefore, rejoice, O heavens! And you who live in the heavens, rejoice! But terror will come on the earth and the sea, for the devil has come down to you in great anger, knowing that he has little time."

The heavenly loud voice continued to shout out. The accuser of believers in Jesus is defeated by "the blood of the Lamb and by their testimony." These Christ followers did not love their lives so much that they refused to die for their faith in Jesus. Those who are in heaven are called to rejoice, but terror is about to come on earth and the sea. The devil is now in a rage. He realizes his time is short and will pour out his wrath on earth as God allows him to.

REFLECT

Think of fellow believers in the world who have been martyred for their faith in Jesus. Thank God that they did not love their lives so much that they were unwilling to die.

RESPOND

Take the time to read Hebrews 11:32-40. Hebrews 11 is considered to be the "Hall of Faith" chapter of the Bible. May it encourage you as you also hear reports of so many being martyred for their faith in modern times.

DAY 3

RECEIVE

Revelation 12:13-14

[13] When the dragon realized that he had been thrown down to the earth, he pursued the woman who had given birth to the male child. [14] But she was given two wings like those of a great eagle so she could fly to the place prepared for her in the wilderness. There she would be cared for and protected from the dragon for a time, times, and half a time.

Although there is debate about who the woman is in Revelation 12, there is no doubt about who the dragon is because he is named as the devil and Satan. Two names for the same person. The Scriptures leave no doubt that Satan is opposed to Jesus Christ. It logically follows that Satan is opposed to the nation of Israel through which Jesus entered into the world. The woman, most likely representing Israel, will be protected for "time, times, and a half a time," another way of saying three and a half years.

REFLECT

In God's sovereign plan He used the nation Israel to bring His Son into the world. Because He is God, Jesus has always existed, but He came in human form when He was born of the virgin Mary in Bethlehem.

RESPOND

To see the deity of Jesus and His humanity in the same verse, check out Isaiah 9:6. A child is born, but a son is given.

REVELATION

DAY 4

RECEIVE

Revelation 12:15-18

¹⁵ Then the dragon tried to drown the woman with a flood of water that flowed from his mouth. ¹⁶ But the earth helped her by opening its mouth and swallowing the river that gushed out from the mouth of the dragon. ¹⁷ And the dragon was angry at the woman and declared war against the rest of her children—all who keep God's commandments and maintain their testimony for Jesus. ¹⁸ Then the dragon took his stand on the shore beside the sea.

A spiritual warfare between God and Satan continues in the Tribulation. Satan causes a flood trying to drown the woman, but God opens the earth and swallows it. Satan becomes even more angry at the woman and "her children." These children would be Jewish people who believe Jesus is the Messiah and maintain their testimony for Him. Then Satan takes his stand on the shore beside the sea. This leads into chapter 13 where Satan's top leader is revealed.

REFLECT

Are you impressed more than ever that Satan never lets up in his desire to persecute Jesus and His people? Satan is under a sentence now and his execution will be carried out in the future.

RESPOND

Read Hebrews 2:14-15 to see what Jesus had to do to break the power of the devil. Rejoice that Jesus provides salvation and spiritual victory to those who believe in Him.

Day 5

RECEIVE

Revelation 13:1-2

¹ Then I saw a beast rising up out of the sea. It had seven heads and ten horns, with ten crowns on its horns. And written on each head were names that blasphemed God. ² This beast looked like a leopard, but it had the feet of a bear and the mouth of a lion! And the dragon gave the beast his own power and throne and great authority.

The "sea" seems to be representative of nations (Gentiles). This beast will be a person who is the head of the revived Roman Empire and known as the "Antichrist." The rulers in this empire blaspheme God. The four beasts referred to in verse 2 are similar to the four mentioned in Daniel 7:4-7. The beast is Satan's main person in the Tribulation to carry out his will.

REFLECT

Be confident that even though Satan seems to have the upper hand at this point in the Tribulation, the main message of Revelation is that God wins.

RESPOND

Read John 16:5-11 that says the ruler of this world (Satan) has already been judged. Jesus spoke these words before He was crucified, rose from the dead and ascended to the Father. Satan's judgment was so certain, however, it was spoken of in the past tense.

WEEK 23: REVELATION 13

RECEIVE

DAY 1

Revelation 13:3-4

³ I saw that one of the heads of the beast seemed wounded beyond recovery—but the fatal wound was healed! The whole world marveled at this miracle and gave allegiance to the beast. ⁴ They worshiped the dragon for giving the beast such power, and they also worshiped the beast. "Who is as great as the beast?" they exclaimed. "Who is able to fight against him?"

This first beast in Revelation 13 is the greater of the two mentioned in the chapter and seems to be the Antichrist. He is empowered by the dragon, identified as the devil or Satan. Note the whole world will worship him. This is satanic worship at its worst. Notice that just as Pharaoh's magicians in Egypt were able to imitate miracles, the world will marvel at the miracles produced by Satan through the Antichrist.

REFLECT

Have you thought about how one distinguishes a false miracle from a true one? It can be tested by the message it gives.

RESPOND

As you study Revelation with a friend, read Deuteronomy 13:1-3 that reveals a miracle should be tested by its message. The message you should compare it with is the Bible.

DAY 2

RECEIVE

Revelation 13:5-7

⁵ Then the beast was allowed to speak great blasphemies against God. And he was given authority to do whatever he wanted for forty-two months. ⁶ And he spoke terrible words of blasphemy against God, slandering his name and his dwelling—that is, those who dwell in heaven. ⁷ And the beast was allowed to wage war against God's holy people and to conquer them. And he was given authority to rule over every tribe and people and language and nation.

The forty-two months mentioned in this passage is three and a half years. This is the last half of the seven-year Tribulation period. God allows the Antichrist to blaspheme Him and all who are in heaven. God even allowed the Antichrist to make war against His people. The Antichrist was also allowed to rule all people on earth.

REFLECT

Be thankful that if you are a believer in Jesus now, you will not be here for the terrible time when the Antichrist is terrorizing and ruling over everyone on earth.

RESPOND

Those who are Christ followers now will be caught up to be with Jesus before the Tribulation begins. See 1 Thessalonians 4:13-18 about the time when believers will be caught up to heaven to meet Jesus in the air. Verse 18 says to comfort each other with these words. It would be no comfort if you thought you would have to go through any part of the Tribulation.

WEEK 23: REVELATION 13

RECEIVE

DAY 3

Revelation 13:8-10

⁸ And all the people who belong to this world worshiped the beast. They are the ones whose names were not written in the Book of Life that belongs to the Lamb who was slaughtered before the world was made. ⁹ Anyone with ears to hear should listen and understand. ¹⁰ Anyone who is destined for prison will be taken to prison. Anyone destined to die by the sword will die by the sword. This means that God's holy people must endure persecution patiently and remain faithful.

During the Tribulation, unbelievers will worship the Antichrist. Unbelievers are those whose names are not in the Book of Life. Those who are believers in Jesus in the midst of this worship of a false god will be persecuted. They are encouraged to patiently endure the persecution and to remain faithful to the Lord Jesus.

REFLECT

Think of what a horrible time this will be for believers in Jesus. Even in the 21st century there are believers being persecuted, but it will be much worse during the Tribulation when the world is worshiping the Antichrist.

RESPOND

Even present-day believers are told how to respond to persecutors. See what Jesus said in Matthew 5:43-45, and what the apostle Paul said in Romans 12:14-15.

DAY 4

RECEIVE

Revelation 13:11-13

¹¹ Then I saw another beast come up out of the earth. He had two horns like those of a lamb, but he spoke with the voice of a dragon. ¹² He exercised all the authority of the first beast. And he required all the earth and its people to worship the first beast, whose fatal wound had been healed. ¹³ He did astounding miracles, even making fire flash down to earth from the sky while everyone was watching.

This second beast is referred to as the false prophet later in the book of Revelation. He directs worship toward the first beast, the Antichrist. The opinion differs on whether the first beast (the Antichrist) was actually killed and rose from the dead. This false prophet will do "astounding miracles." Satan does all he can by empowering the Antichrist and false prophet to deceive people.

REFLECT

Surely this is another lesson not to believe everything that seems to be supernatural.

RESPOND

See Revelation 16:13; 19:20; and 20:10 for references to the second beast being referred to as the "false prophet."

WEEK 23: REVELATION 13

DAY 5

RECEIVE

Revelation 13:14-15

¹⁴ And with all the miracles he was allowed to perform on behalf of the first beast, he deceived all the people who belong to this world. He ordered the people to make a great statue of the first beast, who was fatally wounded and then came back to life. ¹⁵ He was then permitted to give life to this statue so that it could speak. Then the statue of the beast commanded that anyone refusing to worship it must die.

This statue of the first beast seems to agree with what is said about the man of lawlessness in 2 Thessalonians 2. In the middle of the seven-year Tribulation the Antichrist will apparently desecrate the temple by placing himself or a statue of himself there to be worshiped. This passage in Revelation reveals somehow the statue will be enabled to speak, and any who will not worship it must die.

REFLECT

Think how terrible it will be to be forced to worship someone or something. This is similar to what Nebuchadnezzar attempted to do with Daniel's three friends (see Daniel 3).

RESPOND

Read 2 Thessalonians 2:3-8 to see what the apostle Paul wrote about the man of lawlessness (the Antichrist) during the Tribulation.

Week 24: Revelation 13, 14

DAY 1

RECEIVE

Revelation 13:16-17

¹⁶ He required everyone—small and great, rich and poor, free and slave—to be given a mark on the right hand or on the forehead. ¹⁷ And no one could buy or sell anything without that mark, which was either the name of the beast or the number representing his name.

The false prophet will require everyone to have the mark of the beast. The mark will be placed on the right hand or on the forehead. Religion will then use economics to enforce its apostate views—no one will be able to buy or sell without having the mark. This will be the means of starving those who refuse to receive the mark and worship the beast. The mark will be "either the name of the beast or the number representing his name."

REFLECT

Think of the believers in Jesus who will be forced to die for their faith for not receiving the mark and worship of the beast.

RESPOND

With a fellow believer, pray for friends and loved ones to trust in Jesus as Savior now so they will never have to face this terrible time.

REVELATION

DAY 2

RECEIVE

Revelation 13:18

¹⁸ Wisdom is needed here. Let the one with understanding solve the meaning of the number of the beast, for it is the number of a man. His number is 666.

This verse says to let one "with understanding solve the meaning of the number of the beast." Those with understanding have been endeavoring to do this for centuries and have suggested various possibilities. Often it seems to them to be someone or some group that is feared the most. It is unlikely anyone will know the true identity until the time comes.

REFLECT

Are you able to concentrate on the portions of the Bible you understand without spending an inordinate time trying to comprehend what is not understandable?

RESPOND

Talk with a Christian friend about being more concerned with a relationship with Jesus now than with what may occur in the future. Read 1 John 2:18-23 to see there are many now who are against Christ (antichrists) even though they are not the Antichrist of the future.

WEEK 24: REVELATION 13, 14

DAY 3

RECEIVE

Revelation 14:1-2

¹ Then I saw the Lamb standing on Mount Zion, and with him were 144,000 who had his name and his Father's name written on their foreheads. ² And I heard a sound from heaven like the roar of mighty ocean waves or the rolling of loud thunder. It was like the sound of many harpists playing together.

The apostle John continues to see the vision revealed to him. The Lamb is the Lord Jesus Christ and Mount Zion is earthly Jerusalem. This seems to be looking ahead to the reign of Jesus on earth. The 144,000 are the ones mentioned in Revelation 7. These have the name of Jesus and His heavenly Father's name written on their foreheads. John hears a loud sound from heaven like the sound of many harpists playing together.

REFLECT

The scene has switched from the horrors brought on by the Antichrist and the false prophet to worship of the Lamb of God. Do you sometimes draw away from other distractions and think only of what the Lord Jesus has done for you?

RESPOND

Focus on the Lord Jesus and what He has done for you by dying in your place, being buried and rising again from the dead. Read 1 Corinthians 15:1-9 to be reminded of these truths and the eyewitnesses who saw Jesus after His resurrection.

RECEIVE

DAY 4

Revelation 14:3-5

³ This great choir sang a wonderful new song in front of the throne of God and before the four living beings and the twenty-four elders. No one could learn this song except the 144,000 who had been redeemed from the earth. ⁴ They have kept themselves as pure as virgins, following the Lamb wherever he goes. They have been purchased from among the people on the earth as a special offering to God and to the Lamb. ⁵ They have told no lies; they are without blame.

Notice that only the 144,000 could learn the wonderful song being sung in front of the throne of God. The 144,000 had kept themselves morally pure when immorality was all around them. Their focus was on following the Lamb, the Lord Jesus Christ. In addition to their pure lives they had integrity—they "told no lies; they are without blame."

REFLECT

Think about your life; can it be said of you that you are morally pure and have integrity? Can people trust whatever you do and say?

RESPOND

Share your concern with a Christian friend about the importance of moral purity and integrity. Read Philippians 1:9-11 to see what Paul prayed for believers in regard to moral purity and integrity.

WEEK 24: REVELATION 13, 14

DAY 5

RECEIVE

Revelation 14:6-7

⁶ And I saw another angel flying through the sky, carrying the eternal Good News to proclaim to the people who belong to this world—to every nation, tribe, language, and people. ⁷ "Fear God," he shouted. "Give glory to him. For the time has come when he will sit as judge. Worship him who made the heavens, the earth, the sea, and all the springs of water."

The word "gospel" literally means "good news." This good news can have various aspects in mind. There is the good news about salvation in Jesus and good news about the kingdom He will eventually establish. Involved in every aspect of good news, however, is the need to be in right relationship with the King, the Lord Jesus. The angel John saw urged people to give glory to Him and worship the creator of everything.

REFLECT

Think what a great God you have. He is the creator of everything yet He loves individuals and loved them so much He was willing to die to pay the penalty for their sins.

RESPOND

When the religious authorities told Peter and John not to speak any longer in the name of Jesus, the disciples said they would obey God rather than man. Persecution could be expected. As the disciples returned to their followers, prayer was fervently made before God. Read Acts 4:23-24 to see how they addressed God in their prayer.

Week 25: Revelation 14

DAY 1

RECEIVE

Revelation 14:8

⁸ Then another angel followed him through the sky, shouting, "Babylon is fallen—that great city is fallen—because she made all the nations of the world drink the wine of her passionate immorality."

Another angel announces that Babylon is fallen. This is given in more detail in Revelation 18. Note the reason for the fall of this great city—"because she made all the nations of the world drink the wine of her passionate immorality." This reveals the extent to which God hates immorality. Some see no problem with it; God sees it as an evil.

REFLECT

Think how the judgment falls on an entire city because of its immorality. What do you see occurring around you? Should where you live be surprised if God's judgment falls?

RESPOND

Take the time to read 1 Corinthians 6:12-20 that tells why believers in Christ should not be involved in sex outside of marriage.

REVELATION

DAY 2

RECEIVE

Revelation 14:9-11

⁹ Then a third angel followed them, shouting, "Anyone who worships the beast and his statue or who accepts his mark on the forehead or on the hand ¹⁰ must drink the wine of God's anger. It has been poured full strength into God's cup of wrath. And they will be tormented with fire and burning sulfur in the presence of the holy angels and the Lamb. ¹¹ The smoke of their torment will rise forever and ever, and they will have no relief day or night, for they have worshiped the beast and his statue and have accepted the mark of his name."

This passage reveals how God's anger will be expressed toward those who worship the beast and his statue and receive his mark. The wine of God's anger will be poured full strength into His cup of wrath. During the Tribulation God will pour out his wrath on those who refuse to worship Him and instead worship Satan's person, the Antichrist. The Christ rejecters will be separated from God forever and they will have no relief day or night.

REFLECT

Think of the serious consequences of denying Jesus as your Savior. The heavenly Father did all He could do in sending His own Son as a sacrifice for sin. Those who refuse the gift of salvation will experience horrible consequences.

RESPOND

Read and think on Romans 5:8 and 6:23. God has done all He can to provide satisfaction for the sins of humanity. Those who refuse to accept the pardon He has offered will have to pay their own penalty.

RECEIVE

DAY 3

Revelation 14:12-13

> [12] This means that God's holy people must endure persecution patiently, obeying his commands and maintaining their faith in Jesus. [13] And I heard a voice from heaven saying, "Write this down: Blessed are those who die in the Lord from now on. Yes, says the Spirit, they are blessed indeed, for they will rest from their hard work; for their good deeds follow them!"

The sobering message for the faithful is that they need to suffer persecution patiently. They are also to obey God's commands and keep their faith in Jesus. A voice from heaven commanded the apostle John to write that those who die in the Lord are blessed. This is especially true during this time of Tribulation, but there are other promises in God's Word about believers who die throughout time.

REFLECT

Do you have loved ones who believed in Jesus and have passed away? They have actually gone to be with Jesus.

RESPOND

Examine verses of comfort for those who have had fellow believers in Jesus pass away. Read and think about Psalm 17:15; 116:15; and John 11:25. For those who sorrow, read Psalm 34:18. These are verses that can be sent to sorrowing loved ones. Select one to send to a friend.

DAY 4

RECEIVE

Revelation 14:14-16

¹⁴ Then I saw a white cloud, and seated on the cloud was someone like the Son of Man. He had a gold crown on his head and a sharp sickle in his hand. ¹⁵ Then another angel came from the Temple and shouted to the one sitting on the cloud, "Swing the sickle, for the time of harvest has come; the crop on earth is ripe." ¹⁶ So the one sitting on the cloud swung his sickle over the earth, and the whole earth was harvested.

A sickle was used for reaping at harvest time to cut the grain. Here the Lord Jesus appears with a sharp sickle to bring judgment. The sickle is swung over the entire earth so it is a worldwide judgment of unbelievers. In coming to the end to the seven-year Tribulation, things are common to what Jesus said as recorded in Matthew 24 and Luke 21.

REFLECT

If you have trusted in Jesus as Savior, you are assured there will be no future judgment for you, as mentioned in John 3:18 and Romans 8:1.

RESPOND

For similarities of Revelation 14:14-16 and what the gospel writers recorded of the words of Jesus, read Matthew 24:30-31 and Luke 21:25-28.

WEEK 25: REVELATION 14

DAY 5

RECEIVE

Revelation 14:17-18

¹⁷ After that, another angel came from the Temple in heaven, and he also had a sharp sickle. ¹⁸ Then another angel, who had power to destroy with fire, came from the altar. He shouted to the angel with the sharp sickle, "Swing your sickle now to gather the clusters of grapes from the vines of the earth, for they are ripe for judgment."

It is impossible to read these passages in Revelation without realizing it will be a terrible time of judgment. There is no way to explain away the overall message of persecution and judgment. Although God is a God of love, He is also a God of justice. The qualities of His nature are clearly seen in the events being revealed to John in his visions as he was on the isle of Patmos.

REFLECT

Do you understand you serve a God of love as well as justice? To fear God is to have reverential fear and respect for Him.

RESPOND

Various passages in Scripture refer to the justice of God. See Hebrews 1:7-9 for what the heavenly Father says about His Son.

Week 26: Revelation 14, 15

RECEIVE

DAY 1

Revelation 14:19-20

[19] So the angel swung his sickle over the earth and loaded the grapes into the great winepress of God's wrath. [20] The grapes were trampled in the winepress outside the city, and blood flowed from the winepress in a stream about 180 miles long and as high as a horse's bridle.

This passage records what an angel was told to do. It is a picture of God pouring out His wrath. This likely has to do with the campaign of Armageddon that climaxes with this battle. The bloody stream will flow for 180 miles. The blood "as high as a horse's bridle" may not be a stream that deep but blood splashing up to a horse's bridle. Whichever the case, there is a massive amount of bloodshed.

REFLECT

Think of what an awful time of warfare this will be.

RESPOND

With a fellow believer talk about how terrible it will be for those who deny God and experience His wrath. Read Hebrews 10:30-31 in this regard.

RECEIVE

DAY 2

Revelation 15:1–2

¹ Then I saw in heaven another marvelous event of great significance. Seven angels were holding the seven last plagues, which would bring God's wrath to completion. ² I saw before me what seemed to be a glass sea mixed with fire. And on it stood all the people who had been victorious over the beast and his statue and the number representing his name. They were all holding harps that God had given them.

These verses introduce the seven last plagues on the earth. They will "bring God's wrath to completion." These verses tell of the apostle John's vision of the followers of God who had not worshiped the beast nor received his mark. God had given them harps and they are about to sing.

REFLECT

Think about how God cares for His own even in the midst of wrath being poured out on the world.

RESPOND

Encourage a fellow believer by reading Isaiah 43:2 to be assured even now that God is with His followers and will help them through the storms of life.

WEEK 26: REVELATION 14, 15

RECEIVE

DAY 3

Revelation 15:3-4

³ And they were singing the song of Moses, the servant of God, and the song of the Lamb: "Great and marvelous are your works, O Lord God, the Almighty. Just and true are your ways, O King of the nations. ⁴ Who will not fear you, Lord, and glorify your name? For you alone are holy. All nations will come and worship before you, for your righteous deeds have been revealed."

With their harps, those believers who had not worshiped the image nor received his mark are now singing the song of Moses and of the Lamb. They praise the Lord for His marvelous works. They praise Him for being the King of all nations. Even though the nations rage against God now they will someday come and worship before Him.

REFLECT

Think how humbling it will be for those nations who reject God and refuse to acknowledge Him now will someday be forced to worship Him.

RESPOND

Read Philippians 2:5-11 to see the attitude Jesus had, which is an example to all believers. He did not think of Himself but others. Someday even unbelievers will bow before Jesus and admit that He is God. Pray that people with trust in Him as Savior now so they are not forced to bow before Him in the future.

REVELATION

RECEIVE

DAY 4

Revelation 15:5-6

⁵ Then I looked and saw that the Temple in heaven, God's Tabernacle, was thrown wide open. ⁶ The seven angels who were holding the seven plagues came out of the Temple. They were clothed in spotless white linen with gold sashes across their chests.

This passage refers to a temple, or tabernacle, in heaven. This heavenly temple has been referred to in the Bible previously. At this time there are seven angels holding seven plagues that are about to be released on the earth. John described what their clothing looked like. Each of the seven angels will bring judgment to the earth.

REFLECT

Think of this passage as giving background of the judgments to be seen in the following chapters in Revelation.

RESPOND

Regarding where the temple in heaven is mentioned previously in the Bible, read Hebrews 8:3-5. Jesus could not be a priest on earth because His human lineage was the tribe of Judah, not the tribe of Levi. He is our heavenly priest, however, as mentioned in Hebrews 3:1-3.

WEEK 26: REVELATION 14, 15

DAY 5

RECEIVE

Revelation 15:7-8

⁷ Then one of the four living beings handed each of the seven angels a gold bowl filled with the wrath of God, who lives forever and ever. ⁸ The Temple was filled with smoke from God's glory and power. No one could enter the Temple until the seven angels had completed pouring out the seven plagues.

A bowl was something that could be easily and quickly poured out. Revelation 16 lists the bowls that bring devastating judgments on the earth. Each bowl was filled with the wrath of God. After the seven angels were each given a bowl, smoke from God's power and glory filled the temple. No one was able to enter the temple until the seven plaques were poured out.

REFLECT

Do you see from this passage that God is still in control? There is no more comforting thought than to realize God is in ultimate control (see Proverbs 21:1).

RESPOND

In reading the Bible, attempt to skip the break in chapter divisions that sometimes interrupt the flow of the content. Chapter and verse divisions were added after the original manuscripts were written. This short chapter of Revelation 15 leads you directly into chapter 16 that tells of the seven plagues.

Week 27: Revelation 16

DAY 1

RECEIVE

Revelation 16:1

¹ Then I heard a mighty voice from the Temple say to the seven angels, "Go your ways and pour out on the earth the seven bowls containing God's wrath."

Seven angels are commanded to pour out their bowls on the earth. The bowls contain God's wrath. He has worked for centuries to draw people to Himself through His goodness in sending His own Son as a sacrifice for sin. That has been largely rejected by those on earth during the Tribulation so now God's wrath is being poured out.

REFLECT

If you have trusted in Jesus for your salvation, you have experienced God's goodness. Think how terrible it will be for those who continue to reject Him.

RESPOND

Do you have a fellow believer to talk with about these matters? Thank God for His goodness and pray for others to see the need to trust in Jesus as Savior.

DAY 2

RECEIVE

Revelation 16:2-3

² So the first angel left the Temple and poured out his bowl on the earth, and horrible, malignant sores broke out on everyone who had the mark of the beast and who worshiped his statue. ³ Then the second angel poured out his bowl on the sea, and it became like the blood of a corpse. And everything in the sea died.

This passage tells of the first two angels who pour out their bowls of the wrath of God. The first one brings malignant sores on all who had the mark of the beast and who worshiped his statue. Taking the mark allowed them to buy and sell; now judgment from God is falling on them. The second angel's bowl of wrath was poured out on the sea, which became like the blood of a dead person. The wrath poured out by the first angel was on those on earth; the second angel's bowl of wrath was on everything in the sea.

REFLECT

All of this you are reading about is directed by the God of the universe. Be thankful that believers in Jesus will not be part of suffering this wrath of God.

RESPOND

Read Exodus 7:14-18 to see when God predicted what He would do to the river Nile in Egypt, worshiped by the Egyptians. That came about, but Pharaoh did not turn to God. In the end of the Tribulation something worse will occur but people still will not turn to God.

WEEK 27: REVELATION 16

DAY 3

RECEIVE

Revelation 16:4-7

⁴ Then the third angel poured out his bowl on the rivers and springs, and they became blood. ⁵ And I heard the angel who had authority over all water saying, "You are just, O Holy One, who is and who always was, because you have sent these judgments. ⁶ Since they shed the blood of your holy people and your prophets, you have given them blood to drink. It is their just reward." ⁷ And I heard a voice from the altar, saying, "Yes, O Lord God, the Almighty, your judgments are true and just."

The bowl of wrath poured out by the second angel was on the sea. The third angel pours out his bowl of wrath on "the rivers and springs." For those who might think this judgment was too harsh, the angel "who had authority over all water" defends God's actions. God is not only loving; He is also holy and just. A voice from the altar addresses God as "the Almighty"; that is, He is mighty over all and His "judgments are true and just."

REFLECT

Consider that the God you serve is almighty over everything and everyone. Thank Him for His power and glory.

RESPOND

Read Genesis 35:9-12 to see the change of Jacob's name and the Hebrew name for "God Almighty."

REVELATION

DAY 4

RECEIVE

Revelation 16:8-9

⁸ Then the fourth angel poured out his bowl on the sun, causing it to scorch everyone with its fire. ⁹ Everyone was burned by this blast of heat, and they cursed the name of God, who had control over all these plagues. They did not repent of their sins and turn to God and give him glory.

The fourth angel poured out his bowl of God's wrath on the sun causing it to scorch everyone on earth. Did this extreme judgment cause people to turn to God? No, they did not repent and turn to Him. Instead they cursed God for this plague. At least they seemed to recognize God was in control of the judgment and that it could not have occurred without Him allowing it.

REFLECT

Even unbelievers sometimes realize that God is in ultimate control. Be thankful you serve such a great God and that as a believer in Jesus you will be blessed and not cursed.

RESPOND

The passage in Revelation tells of future judgment for unbelievers. Read Matthew 11:20-24 to see the judgment Jesus pronounced on unbelievers during His time on earth.

WEEK 27: REVELATION 16

DAY 5

RECEIVE

Revelation 16:10-11

¹⁰ Then the fifth angel poured out his bowl on the throne of the beast, and his kingdom was plunged into darkness. His subjects ground their teeth in anguish, ¹¹ and they cursed the God of heaven for their pains and sores. But they did not repent of their evil deeds and turn to God.

Now judgment is poured out on the throne of the Antichrist. Darkness enveloped his kingdom. God is light, as mentioned in 1 John 1:5. The darkness in the empire of the beast is an indication of the absence of God. As the subjects of the Antichrist were in pain, they cursed God for their pain and sores. Their greatest need was to turn to God, but they did not.

REFLECT

Think how wonderful it is that you can serve the God of light rather than darkness. May you be used of God to tell others of your faith in Jesus so they, too, can turn to the God of light.

RESPOND

For another example of how God brought darkness on unbelievers, read Exodus 10:21-23. This judgment did not cause Pharaoh to turn to God, just as in the Tribulation it will not cause unbelievers to turn to God.

WEEK 28: REVELATION 16

RECEIVE

DAY 1

Revelation 16:12

¹² Then the sixth angel poured out his bowl on the great Euphrates River, and it dried up so that the kings from the east could march their armies toward the west without hindrance.

This prophecy reveals the alignment of armies leading to the final great conflict. These "kings from the east" will march their armies toward Israel. This is all in preparation for the last great world war. Even now there have been dams constructed, but this verse indicates it will be a supernatural event. It is typical of God-deniers to endeavor to explain everything apart from a miracle-working God.

REFLECT

Even though there are natural means for many things, are you confident God can work miracles when He desires to?

RESPOND

As you examine these verses in Revelation 16 you are viewing the events leading up to the second coming of the Lord Jesus Christ to the earth. Share these with a fellow believer.

DAY 2

RECEIVE

Revelation 16:13-14

¹³ And I saw three evil spirits that looked like frogs leap from the mouths of the dragon, the beast, and the false prophet. ¹⁴ They are demonic spirits who work miracles and go out to all the rulers of the world to gather them for battle against the Lord on that great judgment day of God the Almighty.

From the previous passages in Revelation, the "dragon" refers to the devil (Revelation 12:9). The beast refers to the Antichrist (Revelation 13:1-3). The false prophet refers to the second beast in Revelation 13:11-13. They will work miracles as they gather armies against the Lord "on that great judgment day of God the Almighty."

REFLECT

These will be terrible times on earth as the Lord readies to bring on the great judgment day.

RESPOND

As you meet with a fellow believer in Jesus, talk about reminding people who are concerned about future events to realize they have no assurance of how long they will live. This is why it is important to trust in Jesus as Savior now. Discuss how you can gently approach this topic with them.

WEEK 28: REVELATION 16

DAY 3

RECEIVE

Revelation 16:15

¹⁵ "Look, I will come as unexpectedly as a thief! Blessed are all who are watching for me, who keep their clothing ready so they will not have to walk around naked and ashamed."

During the Church age, as well as in the future Tribulation, there are warnings for people to be on the watch for the Lord's return. A thief comes unexpectedly and many will not be ready when the Lord returns. This verse in Revelation is warning those near the end of the seven-year Tribulation not to be caught off guard when the Lord returns to earth. The clothing mentioned may refer to the righteous acts of the saints (see Revelation 19:7-8).

REFLECT

Are you prepared if the Lord should appear in the sky to catch up believers to Himself? Believers in Jesus should live as if He could come back at any time.

RESPOND

Read 2 Peter 3:9-11 to see the warning the apostle gave about what will occur at the end of the age and how it should affect our lives now.

DAY 4

RECEIVE

Revelation 16:16

¹⁶ And the demonic spirits gathered all the rulers and their armies to a place with the Hebrew name Armageddon.

"Armageddon" refers to the mountain of Megiddo. This is thought to be on the plain of Esdraelon, which Napoleon thought was a perfect battlefield. The focus is against Israel because Satan and his demons have always wanted to destroy Israel through whom the Messiah came. They failed in His first advent and are still trying to destroy Israel before His second advent.

REFLECT

Think of how much Satan despises the Lord Jesus Christ because Satan wants to be worshiped instead of Him.

RESPOND

Read Matthew 4:8-9 to see that Satan, also known as the devil, wanted Jesus to worship him. Read verse 10 to see what Jesus answered.

WEEK 28: REVELATION 16

DAY 5

RECEIVE

Revelation 16:17-18

¹⁷ Then the seventh angel poured out his bowl into the air. And a mighty shout came from the throne in the Temple, saying, "It is finished!" ¹⁸ Then the thunder crashed and rolled, and lightning flashed. And a great earthquake struck—the worst since people were placed on the earth.

As the seventh angel poured out his bowl judgment, a mighty shout from heaven exclaimed, "It is finished!" This brought the seven bowl judgments to an end. The Lord is about to appear but before He does other events will take place. The thunder crashed and rolled and lightning flashed, and there was a great earthquake such as there had never been.

REFLECT

Consider the signs in the sky that will accompany these end time events. Even nature will seem to be in an upheaval.

RESPOND

Read Luke 21:7-11 to see what Jesus predicted about the end times when His disciples asked Him about that time. Those who know Jesus as Savior now will be caught up to heaven before that time (see 1 Thessalonians 4:13-18).

Week 29: Revelation 16, 17

DAY 1

RECEIVE

Revelation 16:19

¹⁹ The great city of Babylon split into three sections, and the cities of many nations fell into heaps of rubble. So God remembered all of Babylon's sins, and he made her drink the cup that was filled with the wine of his fierce wrath.

Some may sin and think God does not know it, but this passage reveals He not only knows it but also remembers the sins. Notice also that "the cities of many nations fell into heaps of rubble." This was the result of the earthquake that was greater than any time people had been on earth. Although God is a God of love, He hates sin and will pour out judgment on the sins of Babylon. Some view rebuilt Babylon on the Euphrates as the center of world government in the Tribulation.

REFLECT

Believers in Jesus can rejoice that God has bought them out of the market place of sin where Satan was their master. Jesus was the sacrifice that made this possible.

RESPOND

With another Christ follower, read Romans 6:5-11 to see what Jesus has done for believers. Be thankful that you are no longer a slave to sin.

REVELATION

DAY 2

RECEIVE

Revelation 16:20-21

[20] And every island disappeared, and all the mountains were leveled. [21] There was a terrible hailstorm, and hailstones weighing as much as seventy-five pounds fell from the sky onto the people below. They cursed God because of the terrible plague of the hailstorm.

This records more results of the earthquake greater than anything seen in world history. Think of the islands disappearing and all mountains being leveled. Think also of the devastation and death the hailstones would cause. One would think in the midst of this that people would begin crying out to God for mercy. Instead, they curse God because of the hailstorm. They seem to have an understanding that God could have stopped it.

REFLECT

As you consider the effects of nature today, do you realize God is in ultimate control? It seems the unbelievers in the Tribulation will understand that.

RESPOND

Read Exodus 9:13-26 to read about the greatest hailstorm to ever hit Egypt. What is recorded in Revelation 16 has an effect on the entire world.

WEEK 29: REVELATION 16, 17

DAY 3

RECEIVE

Revelation 17:1-2

¹ One of the seven angels who had poured out the seven bowls came over and spoke to me. "Come with me," he said, "and I will show you the judgment that is going to come on the great prostitute, who rules over many waters. ² The kings of the world have committed adultery with her, and the people who belong to this world have been made drunk by the wine of her immorality."

Revelation 17 seems to refer to the judgment on religious Babylon and Revelation 18 on commercial Babylon. A spiritual prostitute is one who had gone to false gods instead of to the true and only God. It seems that immorality is what accompanies the worship of false gods. Here the "kings of the world have committed adultery with her." This reveals a political marriage with an apostate religious system.

REFLECT

Always be on guard when you see a political government becoming involved with religious life. The end result is usually not good.

RESPOND

Both Egypt with its pharaohs and Rome with its emperors confused political leaders with religious leaders. Even the plagues of Egypt were directed against what was thought divine in the land, such as the pharaohs and the river Nile. God revealed He was greater than any god the Egyptians worshiped.

REVELATION

DAY 4

RECEIVE

Revelation 17:3-4

³ So the angel took me in the Spirit into the wilderness. There I saw a woman sitting on a scarlet beast that had seven heads and ten horns, and blasphemies against God were written all over it. ⁴ The woman wore purple and scarlet clothing and beautiful jewelry made of gold and precious gems and pearls. In her hand she held a gold goblet full of obscenities and the impurities of her immorality.

These verses seem to indicate a dominance of the apostate religious system over the beast (the Antichrist) at this time. Likely this refers to the first half of the seven-year Tribulation. The woman is seen in beautiful dress and ornaments but as being full of "obscenities and the impurities of her immorality."

REFLECT

Think how often the world tries to cover up its sinful acts with outward allurements.

RESPOND

Read Galatians 5:19-21 to see what occurs when people follow the desires of their sinful nature. Make it your desire to honor Jesus Christ in your life.

WEEK 29: REVELATION 16, 17

DAY 5

RECEIVE

Revelation 17:5-6

⁵ A mysterious name was written on her forehead: "Babylon the Great, Mother of All Prostitutes and Obscenities in the World."
⁶ I could see that she was drunk—drunk with the blood of God's holy people who were witnesses for Jesus. I stared at her in complete amazement.

In his vision the apostle John saw a name on the forehead of the woman: "Babylon the Great, Mother of All Prostitutes and Obscenities in the World." What a horrible descriptive name. John also saw that she was drunk with "the blood of God's holy people who were witnesses for Jesus." This reveals that the apostate religious system will consider believers in Jesus to be a chief enemy. Although the false system cannot destroy God, it will seek to destroy His followers.

REFLECT

This name is what the woman was known as. How would you like to be known by others?

RESPOND

With another Christ follower read 2 Timothy 1:1-5 that tells how Paul remembered Timothy. Live in such a way that others can say similar things about you.

Week 30: Revelation 17

DAY 1

RECEIVE

Revelation 17:7-8

⁷ "Why are you so amazed?" the angel asked. "I will tell you the mystery of this woman and of the beast with seven heads and ten horns on which she sits. ⁸ The beast you saw was once alive but isn't now. And yet he will soon come up out of the bottomless pit and go to eternal destruction. And the people who belong to this world, whose names were not written in the Book of Life before the world was made, will be amazed at the reappearance of this beast who had died."

The angel did not understand why John was so perplexed about the woman mentioned in the previous verses. Many think the references in these verses are to the Roman empire and its various emperors. John had been exiled to the island of Patmos by Domitian. It is assumed there will be a revived Roman empire at the time of the Tribulation and that Satan's person, the Antichrist, will be the chief ruler over all others.

REFLECT

Although uncertain about many of the details, you can be sure that in the future there will be much more Satanic activity than we see even now.

RESPOND

Revelation 17:8 indicates unbelievers "will be amazed" at these supernatural events. Read 2 Thessalonians 2:9-12 that also tells about the Antichrist and those who will be deceived by him.

DAY 2

RECEIVE

Revelation 17:9-10

⁹ "This calls for a mind with understanding: The seven heads of the beast represent the seven hills where the woman rules. They also represent seven kings. ¹⁰ Five kings have already fallen, the sixth now reigns, and the seventh is yet to come, but his reign will be brief."

The angel now identifies for John who is referred to by the seven heads of the beast. They represent "the seven hills where the woman rules." Some take this as a reference to the city of Rome, which was considered to be on seven hills. The angel goes on to say, however, they also represent "seven kings." This could refer to the emperors of the Roman empire. Five were already in the past and the sixth that rules at the time would be a reference to Domitian who had exiled John to Patmos. The seventh beast is not identified here.

REFLECT

In considering the book of Revelation, it may be difficult to determine exactly who is referred to by the people and events. Remember, however, that God is in ultimate control and this is a preparation for the return of Jesus to the earth.

RESPOND

With a friend, take the time to read Revelation 6:9-11 that tells of the souls of martyrs crying out to the "sovereign Lord." In times of persecution it is comforting to know that God is sovereign. Talk about world problems today and be reminded that God is in ultimate control over all.

WEEK 30: REVELATION 17

DAY 3

RECEIVE

Revelation 17:11-12

¹¹ "The scarlet beast that was, but is no longer, is the eighth king. He is like the other seven, and he, too, is headed for destruction. ¹² The ten horns of the beast are ten kings who have not yet risen to power. They will be appointed to their kingdoms for one brief moment to reign with the beast."

Now the eighth king is mentioned. He will rule over ten other kings who will rise to power. Their strength may be impressive at the time but their rule will be short-lived. They will reign with the beast but all are headed to defeat.

REFLECT

Does this help you to see that no matter how powerful unbelievers and kingdoms appear for a time, God will have the ultimate say and judgment of them?

RESPOND

Read Daniel 7:7-9 that tells of ten horns and a little horn boasting arrogantly until the Lord returns.

REVELATION

DAY 4

RECEIVE

Revelation 17:13–14

¹³ "They will all agree to give him their power and authority. ¹⁴ Together they will go to war against the Lamb, but the Lamb will defeat them because he is Lord of all lords and King of all kings. And his called and chosen and faithful ones will be with him."

The ten kings will join with the beast in making war against the Lamb. It seems as if this cannot possibly be an equal battle with ten kings against a lamb. The Lamb defeats them, however, when He returns "because he is Lord of all lords and King of all kings." Note that Jesus has believers with Him at this time.

REFLECT

A great assurance of every believer is that he or she is in the care of the Lord Jesus Christ no matter what period of time is involved.

RESPOND

At the rapture of the saints, mentioned in 1 Thessalonians 4:13–18, Jesus comes "for" believers. At His second advent to the earth He will come "with" His saints, as Revelation 17:14 says.

WEEK 30: REVELATION 17

DAY 5

RECEIVE

Revelation 17:15-16

[15] Then the angel said to me, "The waters where the prostitute is ruling represent masses of people of every nation and language. [16] The scarlet beast and his ten horns all hate the prostitute. They will strip her naked, eat her flesh, and burn her remains with fire."

Verse 15 reveals "waters" represent all of humanity. Here the beast will hate the prostitute and devour her. It seems the prostitute, representing the apostate church, dominates the beast in the first half of the Tribulation, but then the beast gains control during the last half of the Tribulation and dominates the apostate church.

REFLECT

This is a reminder to realize that when the church and government are intertwined, the government usually dominates. It certainly will in the Tribulation.

RESPOND

Talk with a Christian friend about always supporting biblical values when they conflict with governmental values.

Week 31: Revelation 17, 18

RECEIVE

DAY 1

Revelation 17:17-18

[17] "For God has put a plan into their minds, a plan that will carry out his purposes. They will agree to give their authority to the scarlet beast, and so the words of God will be fulfilled. [18] And this woman you saw in your vision represents the great city that rules over the kings of the world."

The angel continues to tell John about the ten kings serving with the scarlet beast. The difference of opinion is over what is "the great city that rules over the kings of the world." Is it Babylon on the Euphrates river with the woman whose headquarters are in Rome? Revelation 18 simply identifies the city as Babylon.

REFLECT

The world religion of the Antichrist will be even worse than the apostate church and its world religion.

RESPOND

Satan has always wanted to be worshiped instead of the Lord Jesus Christ. Satan's main person, the Antichrist, will carry out his desire. Read 2 Thessalonians 2:3-4 to see what the Antichrist will do during the Tribulation.

RECEIVE

DAY 2

Revelation 18:1-2

¹ After all this I saw another angel come down from heaven with great authority, and the earth grew bright with his splendor. ² He gave a mighty shout: "Babylon is fallen—that great city is fallen! She has become a home for demons. She is a hideout for every foul spirit, a hideout for every foul vulture and every foul and dreadful animal."

The brilliant appearance of this angel lightens up the earth, which must have been a startling sight. His mighty shout declared that "Babylon is fallen." The great city will be known as a home for demons and unclean spirits and detestable animals. This is the center of the political and commercial world during the last half of the Tribulation. Revelation 17 revealed judgment on religious Babylon; Revelation 18 is the judgment on political and commercial Babylon.

REFLECT

For those who think they will escape judgment, Revelation 17 and 18 show otherwise.

RESPOND

Read Romans 1:18-20 to see that God's judgment falls on those who reject Him. Pray for friends to trust in Him as Savior now.

WEEK 31: REVELATION 17, 18

DAY 3

RECEIVE

Revelation 18:3-4

³ "For all the nations have fallen because of the wine of her passionate immorality. The kings of the world have committed adultery with her. Because of her desires for extravagant luxury, the merchants of the world have grown rich." ⁴ Then I heard another voice calling from heaven, "Come away from her, my people. Do not take part in her sins, or you will be punished with her."

This passage reveals the world has become rich through its relationship with Babylon and all the immorality associated with it. Those relative few who love the Lord are called out of Babylon and told not to take part in her sins. Throughout time, God has urged believers to live apart from the sins of unbelievers.

REFLECT

Each person lives surrounded by immorality. Do you have the desire to live completely apart from any of that contamination?

RESPOND

Read 2 Corinthians 6:14-18 to see God's appeal for believers to be separate from the immoral lives of unbelievers.

DAY 4

RECEIVE

Revelation 18:5-6

⁵ "For her sins are piled as high as heaven, and God remembers her evil deeds. ⁶ Do to her as she has done to others. Double her penalty for all her evil deeds. She brewed a cup of terror for others, so brew twice as much for her."

The voice from heaven continues calling out. The evaluation of Babylon is that God remembers all of her evil deeds. The voice calls out for God to double her penalty for all she has done. Because the city has been guilty of what she has done to others, the voice calls out for God to do twice as much to her.

REFLECT

No one can hide sins from God. He knows all that is going on and remembers the evil thoughts and actions of those who reject His Son as Savior.

RESPOND

With a fellow believer talk about how God has removed sin from those who believe in Jesus as Savior. Read Psalm 103:10-12 to see that sins are removed from believers as far as the east is from the west. One can go so far north that he will begin going south, but he can never go so far east that he begins going west. That's how far God has removed sins from the believer.

WEEK 31: REVELATION 17, 18

DAY 5

RECEIVE

Revelation 18:7-8

⁷ "She glorified herself and lived in luxury, so match it now with torment and sorrow. She boasted in her heart, 'I am queen on my throne. I am no helpless widow, and I have no reason to mourn.' ⁸ Therefore, these plagues will overtake her in a single day—death and mourning and famine. She will be completely consumed by fire, for the Lord God who judges her is mighty."

The voice from heaven continues to tell about Babylon and the way the city lived in luxury and the nations profited from her. Those in the city lived as if they would never have to face judgment, but now it will come in one day. The city will experience death, mourning and famine. The Lord will consume the city by fire.

REFLECT

The events now being read about in Revelation 18 will be associated with the return of the Lord Jesus to earth.

RESPOND

The wicked will have their part in the lake of fire, called the "second death" in Revelation 2:11; 20:6, 14; 21:8. Those who have trusted in Jesus for salvation will never experience the awful consequences of this death.

Week 32: Revelation 18

RECEIVE

DAY 1

Revelation 18:9-10

⁹ And the kings of the world who committed adultery with her and enjoyed her great luxury will mourn for her as they see the smoke rising from her charred remains. ¹⁰ They will stand at a distance, terrified by her great torment. They will cry out, "How terrible, how terrible for you, O Babylon, you great city! In a single moment God's judgment came on you."

The voice from heaven continued with this announcement about Babylon. The commercial world has prospered from the city's wickedness and now it is mourning her destruction. At least the people realize the judgment on the city is from God and not from natural circumstances. Secular humanism has no room for God but these kings and merchants know who is bringing judgment.

REFLECT

How do you think of circumstances around you? Do you realize God is in ultimate control and that these events could not occur unless He allowed them?

RESPOND

Meet with a friend to talk about difficult circumstances. Read 1 Thessalonians 5:18 and Romans 8:28. Notice instructions in 1 Thessalonians 5:18 are not to be thankful "for" everything but "in" everything. Realize from Romans 8:28 each circumstance may not be good but when worked together with others it will be for your ultimate good and God's glory.

DAY 2

RECEIVE

Revelation 18:11-12

¹¹ The merchants of the world will weep and mourn for her, for there is no one left to buy their goods. ¹² She bought great quantities of gold, silver, jewels, and pearls; fine linen, purple, silk, and scarlet cloth; things made of fragrant thyine wood, ivory goods, and objects made of expensive wood; and bronze, iron, and marble.

Notice the merchants are mourning that there is no one left to buy their goods. There is no indication they are mourning over the wickedness of the city but only because of their monetary loss. Then a list is given of the many items that were bought by those in the city of Babylon. Remember, as the city is referred to it is referring to the people in it.

REFLECT

Just as when Babylon is mentioned it is referring to the people in it; do you realize when the "world" is mentioned in the Bible it is referring to the people?

RESPOND

Be reminded of the truth you are reflecting on by reading John 1:10-13; 3:16-17; 12:46-48.

WEEK 32: REVELATION 18

DAY 3

RECEIVE

Revelation 18:13-14

¹³ She also bought cinnamon, spice, incense, myrrh, frankincense, wine, olive oil, fine flour, wheat, cattle, sheep, horses, wagons, and bodies—that is, human slaves. ¹⁴ "The fancy things you loved so much are gone," they cry. "All your luxuries and splendor are gone forever, never to be yours again."

This passage continues a list of items those in Babylon bought and made the merchants rich. Notice they even bought human slaves. When wealth is the main concern, even people are treated as objects. The merchants are not grieving over the bad human conditions but over their loss of wealth.

REFLECT

How is it with you? Is your mind more on luxuries than on the needs of your fellow human beings? Some of the saddest slavery today is the sex trafficking done by criminals.

RESPOND

Talk with a friend about how the focus on material gain can be a detriment. See passages such as Matthew 6:24; 2 Corinthians 4:17-18; and 1 Timothy 6:9-10. These passages will provide much food for thought as you wish to honor the Lord with your life and pocket book.

REVELATION

DAY 4

RECEIVE

Revelation 18:15–17

> [15] The merchants who became wealthy by selling her these things will stand at a distance, terrified by her great torment. They will weep and cry out, [16] "How terrible, how terrible for that great city! She was clothed in finest purple and scarlet linens, decked out with gold and precious stones and pearls! [17] In a single moment all the wealth of the city is gone!" And all the captains of the merchant ships and their passengers and sailors and crews will stand at a distance.

The merchants who prospered from the wealth of the people of Babylon are terrified by the great torment of the city. Although the city had all the outward appearances of wealth and beauty, inwardly she was stricken with spiritual poverty and ungodliness. All that could now be done was for the captains of the merchant ships and passengers to stare from a distance.

REFLECT

Do you realize that outward beauty is not nearly as important to God as inner beauty?

RESPOND

Read about David being chosen to succeed King Saul. The passage is found in 1 Samuel 16:1–13. Although the outer appearance was not as important as the inner heart for God, David was a handsome young man.

WEEK 32: REVELATION 18

DAY 5

RECEIVE

Revelation 18:18-20

[18] They will cry out as they watch the smoke ascend, and they will say, "Where is there another city as great as this?" [19] And they will weep and throw dust on their heads to show their grief. And they will cry out, "How terrible, how terrible for that great city! The shipowners became wealthy by transporting her great wealth on the seas. In a single moment it is all gone." [20] Rejoice over her fate, O heaven and people of God and apostles and prophets! For at last God has judged her for your sakes.

This passage reveals how heartbroken unbelievers are when the source of their earthly gains is gone. They "weep and throw dust on their heads to show their grief." Those are the actions of people who repent of their sins, but these are only feeling sorry for themselves because of the loss of their luxuries. There is no turning to God for help.

REFLECT

Do you also know of some who care more about their earthly life than their eternal life? All unbelievers need to change their thinking in this regard.

RESPOND

There are other examples in the book of Revelation of those who did not repent when things because more difficult for them. Read Revelation 9:20-21; 16:8-11. To "repent" is to change one's mind that brings a change of behavior, but that is not seen in these instances.

Week 33: Revelation 18, 19

Day 1

RECEIVE

Revelation 18:21-22

²¹ Then a mighty angel picked up a boulder the size of a huge millstone. He threw it into the ocean and shouted, "Just like this, the great city Babylon will be thrown down with violence and will never be found again. ²² The sound of harps, singers, flutes, and trumpets will never be heard in you again. No craftsmen and no trades will ever be found in you again. The sound of the mill will never be heard in you again."

The merchants of the world have been grieving over the destruction of the wicked city bringing them phenomenal profits. Now a mighty angel shouted that the city would be thrown down like a huge millstone. The city is to fall down never to be found again. All the sounds that were so welcoming to the merchants and traders are to be no more.

REFLECT

What a lesson to learn that someday this world's goods will be burned. This shows the importance of focusing on that which is eternal rather than on that which is temporal.

RESPOND

In contrasting the eternal with the temporal, read 2 Corinthians 4:17-18 and 2 Peter 3:8-13. Talk to a friend about these passages.

REVELATION

RECEIVE

DAY 2

Revelation 18:23-24

23 "The light of a lamp will never shine in you again. The happy voices of brides and grooms will never be heard in you again. For your merchants were the greatest in the world, and you deceived the nations with your sorceries. 24 In your streets flowed the blood of the prophets and of God's holy people and the blood of people slaughtered all over the world."

The mighty angel continues telling what will occur to the city of Babylon when it is destroyed. The merchants "were the greatest in the world," but had been deceived by the conduct of this wicked city. The Greek word translated "sorceries" is *pharmakeia* from which the word "pharmacy" is derived that refers to drugs. This is an indication that the drug culture will be even more prevalent in the end times than it is now. The anti-God policies are seen by the blood of believers shed all over the world.

REFLECT

Rejoice that as a believer in Jesus you do not need to yield to the desires of the old nature.

RESPOND

Talk with a fellow believer about some of the desires of the old nature. Notice in Galatians 5:19-21 that "sorcery" is mentioned, which refers to drugs.

WEEK 33: REVELATION 18, 19

DAY 3

RECEIVE

Revelation 19:1–2

¹ After this, I heard what sounded like a vast crowd in heaven shouting, "Praise the Lord! Salvation and glory and power belong to our God. ² His judgments are true and just. He has punished the great prostitute who corrupted the earth with her immorality. He has avenged the murder of his servants."

There were no chapter divisions when this was originally written. From the destruction of Babylon it immediately goes on to "After this." The expression "Praise the Lord" is seen in the Hebrew word "hallelujah." Because there was no "h" in Greek it is sometimes translated as "Allelujah." Praise is in the first part of the word and "jah" refers to God. The praise is for God's "salvation and glory and power." These verses continue to view Babylon as the "great prostitute who corrupted the earth with her immorality."

REFLECT

Think of the great contrast between the evils of Babylon and the salvation, glory and power of God.

RESPOND

The book of Psalms ends with what are called the "Hallelujah Psalms." Read the first verses of Psalms 146-150. The psalmist David was full of praise as he wrote these songs that were set to the accompaniment of stringed instruments.

REVELATION

RECEIVE

DAY 4

Revelation 19:3-4

³ And again their voices rang out: "Praise the Lord! The smoke from that city ascends forever and ever!" ⁴ Then the twenty-four elders and the four living beings fell down and worshiped God, who was sitting on the throne. They cried out, "Amen! Praise the Lord!"

The vast crowd in heaven continued their praise of God. Again the expression "Praise the Lord!" There was rejoicing because the "smoke from the city ascends forever and ever." The twenty-four elders seem to represent Church-age saints (see Revelation 4:1-4). They and the "four living beings fell down and worshiped God." They cried out "Amen" which means "so be it" or "agreed," and they also exclaim "Praise the Lord."

REFLECT

When someone else praises the Lord, are you able to agree by saying "Amen"? Some are reluctant to do this but it only means you are agreeing.

RESPOND

With a friend look at the last couple of verses in Paul's letters from Romans to Philemon. In some translations he ends each one with "Amen."

WEEK 33: REVELATION 18, 19

DAY 5

RECEIVE

Revelation 19:5-6

⁵ And from the throne came a voice that said, "Praise our God, all his servants, all who fear him, from the least to the greatest." ⁶ Then I heard again what sounded like the shout of a vast crowd or the roar of mighty ocean waves or the crash of loud thunder: "Praise the Lord! For the Lord our God, the Almighty, reigns."

A voice calls out from heaven for all who fear God, from the least to the greatest, to praise God. This reveals it is not just super saints who should praise Him but even those who only have an elementary knowledge of Him. There is hopefully growth in the Christian life, but even those who do not have it but have trusted in Him as Savior should praise Him. The passage ends with the reason to praise Him: because "the Lord our God, the Almighty, reigns."

REFLECT

Does this help you realize that no matter where you are in the Christian life you can praise the Lord who is Almighty and reigns over everything?

RESPOND

Talk with a Christian friend about being sure to praise God as you think of Him. "Worship" is thinking of God's "worth." When you do this you are worshiping Him. This makes it easy to praise Him.

Week 34: Revelation 19

RECEIVE

DAY 1

Revelation 19:7-8

> ⁷ "Let us be glad and rejoice, and let us give honor to him. For the time has come for the wedding feast of the Lamb, and his bride has prepared herself. ⁸ She has been given the finest of pure white linen to wear." For the fine linen represents the good deeds of God's holy people.

It seems the "bride" refers to the Church-age believers. The Bible distinguishes between the Church, Israel and the Gentiles (see 1 Corinthians 10:32). Dressed in the "finest of pure white linen" represents "the good deeds of God's holy people." This is not just a usual wedding feast; it is "the wedding feast of the Lamb." The Son of God is the bridegroom in this wedding feast.

REFLECT

Think about the wonderful time it will be when believers gather with the Son of God at the wedding feast of the Lamb. The Lamb is the Lord Jesus Christ Himself.

RESPOND

A Christian marriage is to be a picture of the bridegroom, Jesus, and His bride, the Church. Read Ephesians 5:25-33 about this relationship and comparison.

DAY 2

RECEIVE

Revelation 19:9-10

> ⁹ And the angel said to me, "Write this: Blessed are those who are invited to the wedding feast of the Lamb." And he added, "These are true words that come from God." ¹⁰ Then I fell down at his feet to worship him, but he said, "No, don't worship me. I am a servant of God, just like you and your brothers and sisters who testify about their faith in Jesus. Worship only God. For the essence of prophecy is to give a clear witness for Jesus."

The apostle John was told what to write and then he fell down to worship the angel. The angel sees himself only as a created being and tells John not to worship him. The instruction, "Worship only God," reveals that only God is worthy of worship. Here is also seen that the purpose of prophecy is to give a witness about Jesus.

REFLECT

Think about the fact that the Old Testament looks ahead to the Lord Jesus Christ and the New Testament looks back to Him.

RESPOND

That only God is to be worshiped is an indication that Jesus is God. In this regard, compare the words of Jesus in Matthew 4:10 and what the heavenly Father says about His Son in Hebrews 1:5-6. That Jesus is to be worshiped proves from the Scriptures that He is God.

WEEK 34: REVELATION 19

DAY 3

RECEIVE

Revelation 19:11-13

¹¹ Then I saw heaven opened, and a white horse was standing there. Its rider was named Faithful and True, for he judges fairly and wages a righteous war. ¹² His eyes were like flames of fire, and on his head were many crowns. A name was written on him that no one understood except himself. ¹³ He wore a robe dipped in blood, and his title was the Word of God.

In Bible times a horse was a military animal. In peacetimes even kings rode on donkeys. This passage refers to the second advent of Jesus. His first advent was when He came to earth by being born of a virgin in Bethlehem; His second advent is when He comes to earth at the end of the seven-year Tribulation. His crowns were kingly crowns (diadems), not just a victor's (*stephanos*) crown. His title "was the Word of God."

REFLECT

Think how wonderful it will be when Jesus returns to earth.

RESPOND

Notice how the last statement in this passage refers to "the Word of God." Jesus is also referred to as the "Word" in John 1:1. Words are used to express oneself and Jesus came to express the heavenly Father. John 1:18 says that Jesus has declared or made known God.

REVELATION

DAY 4

RECEIVE

Revelation 19:14-16

¹⁴ The armies of heaven, dressed in the finest of pure white linen, followed him on white horses. ¹⁵ From his mouth came a sharp sword to strike down the nations. He will rule them with an iron rod. He will release the fierce wrath of God, the Almighty, like juice flowing from a winepress. ¹⁶ On his robe at his thigh was written this title: King of all kings and Lord of all lords.

This is another contrast regarding believers and Jesus. At the rapture (see 1 Thessalonians 4:13-18), Jesus comes for His saints. At His second advent to earth He comes with His saints. As the "Word" He was able to speak the world into existence; at the end of the Tribulation He will speak armies out of existence. He will rule with a rod of iron and release the wrath of God on unbelievers. No one will doubt then that He is the "King of all kings and Lord of all lords."

REFLECT

Does this passage help you to see how powerful the Lord Jesus Christ is? How does this thought affect your life?

RESPOND

People often pray, "Thy kingdom come Thy will be done on earth as it is in heaven" (see Matthew 6:10). That prayer is being answered in Revelation 19. The following chapter will tell of His rule on earth for 1000 years.

WEEK 34: REVELATION 19

DAY 5

RECEIVE

Revelation 19:17-18

¹⁷ Then I saw an angel standing in the sun, shouting to the vultures flying high in the sky: "Come! Gather together for the great banquet God has prepared. ¹⁸ Come and eat the flesh of kings, generals, and strong warriors; of horses and their riders; and of all humanity, both free and slave, small and great."

There was a wedding feast of the Lamb for believers. This passage reveals a feast for vultures of the sky to come to the feast of dead bodies of unbelievers. This will be a terrible time of destruction for the armies of the world who have opposed the Lord Jesus Christ.

REFLECT

Rejoice if you know Jesus as Savior that you will never have to experience such an awful time.

RESPOND

With a fellow believer, read Zechariah 14:1-5 that tells of the Lord's return to earth. Compare Acts 1:9-12 to see that Jesus will return to the same spot from which He left the earth.

Week 35: Revelation 19, 20

DAY 1

RECEIVE

Revelation 19:19

¹⁹ Then I saw the beast and the kings of the world and their armies gathered together to fight against the one sitting on the horse and his army.

As referred to in Revelation 13, the "beast" is the Antichrist. He seems to be over all the kings and armies of the world and at the end gathers them all to fight against the Lord Jesus Christ. The outcome will not be good for the wicked kings and armies.

REFLECT

No one or army is able to conquer the Lord Jesus Christ and His army. He is Almighty God.

RESPOND

Return to Revelation 13 to read about the beast (Antichrist) in verses 1-8. At that time no one was able to wage war against Him but things change at the second advent of Jesus.

DAY 2

RECEIVE

Revelation 19:20-21

²⁰ And the beast was captured, and with him the false prophet who did mighty miracles on behalf of the beast—miracles that deceived all who had accepted the mark of the beast and who worshiped his statue. Both the beast and his false prophet were thrown alive into the fiery lake of burning sulfur. ²¹ Their entire army was killed by the sharp sword that came from the mouth of the one riding the white horse. And the vultures all gorged themselves on the dead bodies.

Not only was the Antichrist captured but so also was the false prophet who performed miracles and deceived those who had the mark of the beast. Both the Antichrist and false prophet are thrown into the "fiery lake of burning sulfur." Their army was killed by the means of the sword coming out of the mouth of the Lord Jesus Christ. As mentioned previously, He had been able to speak worlds into existence and now was able to speak armies out of existence.

REFLECT

Think of the power of the Lord Jesus Christ in overcoming armies with His spoken word.

RESPOND

With a friend, read Hebrews 4:12-13 to see the power of the Word of God that we know as the Bible. Read also Psalm 139:23-24 and make that your prayer.

WEEK 35: REVELATION 19, 20

DAY 3

RECEIVE

Revelation 20:1-3

¹ Then I saw an angel coming down from heaven with the key to the bottomless pit and a heavy chain in his hand. ² He seized the dragon—that old serpent, who is the devil, Satan—and bound him in chains for a thousand years. ³ The angel threw him into the bottomless pit, which he then shut and locked so Satan could not deceive the nations anymore until the thousand years were finished. Afterward he must be released for a little while.

Revelation 12:7-9 identifies the "dragon" as described in this passage. The dragon is the devil who energizes and empowers the beast and false prophet in opposition to the Lord Jesus Christ. The devil will be bound for a thousand years during which he will not be able to deceive the nations. A Latin term "millennium" is often used in referring to the thousand years. Some take the term as symbolic. This period of time is mentioned six times in Revelation 20:2-7. There is no reason not to accept it as actual years.

REFLECT

Think how wonderful it will be that the devil will be confined for a thousand years so he cannot deceive nations during this time.

RESPOND

The term "kingdom" is also used to refer to the thousand years mentioned in this passage. Isaiah writes about the kingdom. See passages Isaiah 11:6-7 and 65:20-25. It is thought that death will only result during this time because of outright rebellion against the King, the Lord Jesus Christ.

REVELATION

RECEIVE

DAY 4

Revelation 20:4

⁴ Then I saw thrones, and the people sitting on them had been given the authority to judge. And I saw the souls of those who had been beheaded for their testimony about Jesus and for proclaiming the word of God. They had not worshiped the beast or his statue, nor accepted his mark on their foreheads or their hands. They all came to life again, and they reigned with Christ for a thousand years.

The apostle John continued to tell what he saw. He saw thrones and those given authority to judge. He saw those martyred because they testified for the Lord Jesus and proclaimed the Word of God. They had also refused to take the mark of the beast. They came back to life and "reigned with Christ for a thousand years."

REFLECT

Think how courageous these martyrs had been during the Tribulation. Many will have died for their faith even before this time comes.

RESPOND

Read Hebrews 11:32-40. This is what the writer summarized after telling of so many who lived by faith. Those in Hebrews 11 seem to be the witnesses referred to in Hebrews 12:1. As originally written there was no chapter break between 11 and 12.

WEEK 35: REVELATION 19, 20

DAY 5

RECEIVE

Revelation 20:5-6

⁵ This is the first resurrection. (The rest of the dead did not come back to life until the thousand years had ended.) ⁶ Blessed and holy are those who share in the first resurrection. For them the second death holds no power, but they will be priests of God and of Christ and will reign with him a thousand years.

The first resurrection refers to all the various resurrections of believers. The second death refers to the resurrection of unbelievers. The unbelievers will not be resurrected until after the thousand years are completed. The believers who are part of the first resurrection will reign with King Jesus a thousand years.

REFLECT

Think of the privilege of reigning with Christ a thousand years. Details are not given but with God it will be a perfect time for everyone.

RESPOND

The apostle Paul also mentioned to Timothy about reigning with Jesus. Read 2 Timothy 2:11-13. Notice also that even if believers are unfaithful, God never is.

WEEK 36: REVELATION 20

DAY 1

RECEIVE

Revelation 20:7-9

⁷ When the thousand years come to an end, Satan will be let out of his prison. ⁸ He will go out to deceive the nations—called Gog and Magog—in every corner of the earth. He will gather them together for battle—a mighty army, as numberless as sand along the seashore. ⁹ And I saw them as they went up on the broad plain of the earth and surrounded God's people and the beloved city. But fire from heaven came down on the attacking armies and consumed them.

Although Satan had been bound for a thousand years so he could not deceive the nations, he is now loosed for a short time. Once again he is able to deceive the nations—all referred to as "Gog and Magog." Apparently many born during the thousand year reign of Christ had not trusted in Him as Savior, and it is from this group that Satan makes up an army. All come against "the beloved city," Jerusalem, but here they meet their defeat.

REFLECT

Think about nearly perfect peace for a thousand years and yet when Satan is loosed he makes up an army of unbelievers to fight against God. A better environment does not change hearts; only the gospel does.

RESPOND

Talk with a Christian friend about the importance of realizing believers serve a holy and just God and no one or no army will ever be greater than He is. To be "almighty" means there is no one greater. Read Genesis 17:1-6 where God calls Himself by this name as He talked with Abram and changed his name to Abraham.

REVELATION

DAY 2

RECEIVE

Revelation 20:10

¹⁰ Then the devil, who had deceived them, was thrown into the fiery lake of burning sulfur, joining the beast and the false prophet. There they will be tormented day and night forever and ever.

The beast and false prophet had been cast into the lake of fire 1000 years earlier (see Revelation 19:20). After the thousand years the devil is thrown in there with them. Some say the effect of the punishment is eternal, and those in the lake of fire will not be tormented forever and ever. Their view is not supported by this verse that says they "will be tormented day and night forever and ever."

REFLECT

It is sad to think about anyone suffering "forever and ever." The only way to avoid this is to trust in the Lord Jesus Christ for salvation.

RESPOND

God did so much by sending His Son to die for the sins of the world. On the cross, Jesus cried out, "My God, my God, why have you abandoned me?" Read Matthew 27:45-46 to learn about the darkness on earth for the last three hours Jesus was on the cross and at the end of this time the Son cried this out to His heavenly Father. After all the Father and Son went through to provide salvation for those who believe, why would they disregard those who refuse to believe in Jesus for salvation?

WEEK 36: REVELATION 20

DAY 3

RECEIVE

Revelation 20:11-12

¹¹ And I saw a great white throne and the one sitting on it. The earth and sky fled from his presence, but they found no place to hide. ¹² I saw the dead, both great and small, standing before God's throne. And the books were opened, including the Book of Life. And the dead were judged according to what they had done, as recorded in the books.

Revelation 20:11-15 tells about the Great White Throne judgment that all unbelievers will stand before and what the results will be. The Book of Life will be opened and unbelievers will be judged "according to what they had done." This indicates degrees of punishment for unbelievers. Not all have been as bad as others, but none has believed in Jesus for salvation and so must pay for their own sins, as Romans 6:23 says.

REFLECT

Think how privileged you are to have heard the message of salvation. But hearing is not enough; a person must believe the message and trust in Jesus Christ as Savior.

RESPOND

With a friend, read Romans 10:14-15 that tells of the need to get the message out to others so they can believe in Jesus.

DAY 4

RECEIVE

Revelation 20:13-14

¹³ The sea gave up its dead, and death and the grave gave up their dead. And all were judged according to their deeds. ¹⁴ Then death and the grave were thrown into the lake of fire. This lake of fire is the second death.

Wherever an unbeliever's remains have gone at death, they will be brought together with the soul to stand before this judgment. The Greek term for "grave" is "hades" where the rich man was in Luke 16. That is a temporary place of torment for unbelievers until it gives up the dead in it to stand before the Great White Throne judgment. This is called "the second death" that is in contrast to the "first resurrection" also seen contrasted in Revelation 20:5-6.

REFLECT

Be thankful that if you have trusted in Jesus for salvation you will have part in the first resurrection and not in the second death.

RESPOND

Consider with a friend that "the lake of fire" is what is commonly referred to as "hell." Hades is only a temporary place waiting for the final time of judgment. It is not purgatory, as the Bible does not teach anything about purgatory.

WEEK 36: REVELATION 20

DAY 5

RECEIVE

Revelation 20:15

¹⁵ And anyone whose name was not found recorded in the Book of Life was thrown into the lake of fire.

What a sad ending to Revelation 20. Those who have rejected the Lord Jesus Christ as Savior do not have their names in the Book of Life. They have chosen to pay for their own sins instead of trusting in Jesus who paid the penalty of sin for them. Jesus offers a pardon, but the pardon must be accepted to be effective.

REFLECT

Think how sad it will be if any of your loved ones do not have their names in the Book of Life.

RESPOND

A believer cannot convert anyone; that is something only the Holy Spirit can do. The believer's responsibility is to share about Jesus so others might know of the need to trust in Him as Savior. Read 1 Peter 3:15-16 that tells how to do this.

WEEK 37: REVELATION 21

DAY 1

RECEIVE

Revelation 21:1-2

¹ Then I saw a new heaven and a new earth, for the old heaven and the old earth had disappeared. And the sea was also gone. ² And I saw the holy city, the new Jerusalem, coming down from God out of heaven like a bride beautifully dressed for her husband.

Instead of the old heaven and the old earth, the apostle John now sees a new heaven and new earth. Instead of an old earth covered by so much water, the new earth will have no sea. John also sees a new Jerusalem coming down from God. It is adorned as a beautiful bride for her husband.

REFLECT

Do not fret if you don't understand all that is happening. The apostle John likely didn't either. He was just explaining what he saw.

RESPOND

With a Christian friend, read 2 Peter 3:12-14. This passage tells what to expect and how knowing this should change the way we live.

REVELATION

RECEIVE

DAY 2

Revelation 21:3-4

³ I heard a loud shout from the throne, saying, "Look, God's home is now among his people! He will live with them, and they will be his people. God himself will be with them. ⁴ He will wipe every tear from their eyes, and there will be no more death or sorrow or crying or pain. All these things are gone forever."

John hears a loud shout from the throne saying "God's home is now among his people." There can be no greater joy than to know God desires to be with His people. In contrast to all that is taking place now in our lifetimes, all of these difficulties will be gone forever. There will never again be tears, death, sorrow or pain.

REFLECT

Think of what a wonderful time it will be in the future for there never to be heartaches and living where God is with you forever.

RESPOND

Death and sorrow have come to our world because of sin. Read Romans 5:12 that tells of the origin of sin in the world. Read Genesis 3:16-18 to see how the curse of sin affected the woman, the man, and the earth.

WEEK 37: REVELATION 21

DAY 3

RECEIVE

Revelation 21:5-7

⁵ And the one sitting on the throne said, "Look, I am making everything new!" And then he said to me, "Write this down, for what I tell you is trustworthy and true." ⁶ And he also said, "It is finished! I am the Alpha and the Omega—the Beginning and the End. To all who are thirsty I will give freely from the springs of the water of life. ⁷ All who are victorious will inherit all these blessings, and I will be their God, and they will be my children."

John is often told to write something down. In contrast to Revelation 10:4 when he was told not to write something down, here he is told again to "write this down." Alpha and Omega are the first and last letters of the Greek alphabet. This expression is used to show that Jesus is "the Beginning and the End." All who are "victorious" will inherit the blessings described. 1 John 5:4-5 reveals that all who believe in Jesus are those who can experience victory.

REFLECT

If you are a believer in Jesus, you are in the group who are victorious and promised "all these blessings." God also promises Christ followers that He will be with them and they will be His children.

RESPOND

Read John 17:6-12 to see what Jesus prayed for His followers before He left them to ascend back to the heavenly Father.

REVELATION

DAY 4

RECEIVE

Revelation 21:8

⁸ "But cowards, unbelievers, the corrupt, murderers, the immoral, those who practice witchcraft, idol worshipers, and all liars—their fate is in the fiery lake of burning sulfur. This is the second death."

Again the "second death" is mentioned relating to those who reject Jesus Christ as Savior. Specific sins are mentioned but the large category of "unbelievers" covers all those who reject the salvation God has offered them through the sacrifice of His Son. This verse refers to those who did not turn to God. Had they turned to God during their lifetimes, they could have had the forgiveness of sin and eternal life He offered.

REFLECT

Perhaps one of these categories mentioned in Revelation 21:8 is what you were like before you trusted Jesus as Savior. Be thankful you made the decision to trust in Jesus before it was eternally too late.

RESPOND

Read 1 Corinthians 6:9-11 to see that some of the Corinthians lived these sinful lifestyles before salvation. What changed them? Not self-reform, but trusting in Jesus as Savior.

WEEK 37: REVELATION 21

DAY 5

RECEIVE

Revelation 21:9

⁹ Then one of the seven angels who held the seven bowls containing the seven last plagues came and said to me, "Come with me! I will show you the bride, the wife of the Lamb."

One of the angels involved with the seven severe judgments on earth now asks John to come with him to be shown "the bride, the wife of the Lamb." There are parallels to the first-century weddings. Couples were betrothed for about a year but did not live together. Then the groom came for the bride (as Jesus did at the rapture referred to in 1 Thessalonians 4:13-18). This was followed by the marriage and the wedding feast. In Revelation 21:9 the Church-age believers are referred to as the "wife of the Lamb."

REFLECT

If you have trusted in Jesus as Savior you are considered in the group called "the bride of Christ." Some day you will be considered the "wife of the Lamb."

RESPOND

Talk about these truths with a fellow believer. Read such passages as 2 Corinthians 11:2 and Ephesians 5:27 to see how Jesus speaks of believers as His bride and the way He wishes to present her.

WEEK 38: REVELATION 21

DAY 1

RECEIVE

Revelation 21:10-11

[10] So he took me in the Spirit to a great, high mountain, and he showed me the holy city, Jerusalem, descending out of heaven from God. [11] It shone with the glory of God and sparkled like a precious stone—like jasper as clear as crystal.

The apostle John mentions he was carried away and saw "the holy city, Jerusalem, descending out of heaven from God." He does not say where it comes down to so that remains uncertain and open to differing opinions. John describes its beauty as it "shone with the glory of God."

REFLECT

All that can be done by mortals at this time is to imagine the plans and beauty God has waiting for those who trust in Jesus as Savior during their lifetimes.

RESPOND

Read Revelation 21:1-2 that mentions the beauty of the New Jerusalem. Be in awe of the beauty God has planned for believers of all the ages.

REVELATION

RECEIVE

DAY 2

Revelation 21:12-14

¹² The city wall was broad and high, with twelve gates guarded by twelve angels. And the names of the twelve tribes of Israel were written on the gates. ¹³ There were three gates on each side—east, north, south, and west. ¹⁴ The wall of the city had twelve foundation stones, and on them were written the names of the twelve apostles of the Lamb.

The mention of the twelve tribes of Israel and their arrangement around the city is a reminder of how God arranged them around the tabernacle in the Old Testament. This is a reference to Israel. The city had twelve foundation stones "and on them were written the names of the twelve apostles of the Lamb." This is a reference to the Church, of which the apostles were its foundation.

REFLECT

Consider that God remembers believing Israelites as well as believing Gentiles during the Church age. God does not forget anyone.

RESPOND

For a reminder of the arrangement of Israelites around the tabernacle, read Numbers 2:1-2, 32-34. Read Acts 2:42 that tells of believers being dependent on the apostles' teaching. Their teaching is recorded in the Bible you can read today.

WEEK 38: REVELATION 21

DAY 3

RECEIVE

Revelation 21:15-17

¹⁵ The angel who talked to me held in his hand a gold measuring stick to measure the city, its gates, and its wall. ¹⁶ When he measured it, he found it was a square, as wide as it was long. In fact, its length and width and height were each 1,400 miles. ¹⁷ Then he measured the walls and found them to be 216 feet thick (according to the human standard used by the angel).

These dimensions of the city have given much speculation about it. We will never fully understand heaven until we get there. Until then we can be content knowing God has prepared a perfect place for us—and enough room for every believer. Rather than being concerned about what we do not fully know about eternity, let us be content to know Jesus has gone to prepare a perfect place for every believer.

REFLECT

Are you content to leave all the unanswered questions about eternity with Jesus? The main concern Jesus had when He lived among men was to warn them to avoid hell, the lake of fire.

RESPOND

Be reminded of what Jesus is doing for believers by reading John 14:1-3. Whatever place He is preparing will be perfect because He is perfect. For those who have had loved ones pass away who were believers in Jesus, it is comforting to realize they are in a perfect place because they are with Jesus.

REVELATION

DAY 4

RECEIVE

Revelation 21:18-20

[18] The wall was made of jasper, and the city was pure gold, as clear as glass. [19] The wall of the city was built on foundation stones inlaid with twelve precious stones: the first was jasper, the second sapphire, the third agate, the fourth emerald, [20] the fifth onyx, the sixth carnelian, the seventh chrysolite, the eighth beryl, the ninth topaz, the tenth chrysoprase, the eleventh jacinth, the twelfth amethyst.

John continues to describe the city. There is uncertainty about the stones but no uncertainty about God preparing a beautiful place for all those in eternity with Him. This also reveals that God is a God of beauty. Even nature that He has created shows us that today. All believers will be awestruck with the beauty God has prepared for them in the heavenly city.

REFLECT

Do you look forward to being with God in eternity? Doing so will help you to endure the trials of this life.

RESPOND

We can appreciate beauty in this life, but read Proverbs 31:29-31 to see what really counts with God.

WEEK 38: REVELATION 21

DAY 5

RECEIVE

Revelation 21:21-27

²¹ The twelve gates were made of pearls—each gate from a single pearl! And the main street was pure gold, as clear as glass. ²² I saw no temple in the city, for the Lord God Almighty and the Lamb are its temple. ²³ And the city has no need of sun or moon, for the glory of God illuminates the city, and the Lamb is its light. ²⁴ The nations will walk in its light, and the kings of the world will enter the city in all their glory. ²⁵ Its gates will never be closed at the end of day because there is no night there. ²⁶ And all the nations will bring their glory and honor into the city. ²⁷ Nothing evil will be allowed to enter, nor anyone who practices shameful idolatry and dishonesty—but only those whose names are written in the Lamb's Book of Life.

In the Old Testament God's presence was evident in the tabernacle and later the temple (see 1 Chronicles 6:31-32). In the New Testament, every believer is a temple of God (see 1 Corinthians 6:18-20). In eternity there will be no need for any temple because "the Lord God Almighty and the Lamb are its temple." The gates of the city are made of pearls and they will never be closed. God is light so there will be no night there. Only those will be there "whose names are written in the Lamb's Book of Life."

REFLECT

Is your name written in the Lamb's book of life? The only way this is possible is by trusting in Jesus as your Savior.

RESPOND

Read 2 Corinthians 6:2 that reminds everyone that the present time is the time to trust in Jesus as Savior. Tomorrow may be eternally too late. No one has the guarantee of being alive tomorrow, and Hebrews 9:27 reminds us that after death comes judgment. There is no second chance after death.

WEEK 39: REVELATION 22

RECEIVE

DAY 1

Revelation 22:1-2

¹ Then the angel showed me a river with the water of life, clear as crystal, flowing from the throne of God and of the Lamb. ² It flowed down the center of the main street. On each side of the river grew a tree of life, bearing twelve crops of fruit, with a fresh crop each month. The leaves were used for medicine to heal the nations.

This passage reveals the beauty of the New Jerusalem. It also reveals God will provide abundantly for all of the inhabitants. The Garden of Eden had its rivers (see Genesis 2:10-14), but nothing like what God will provide in the future. It should be comforting for every believer to know God will make all things beautiful in eternity.

REFLECT

What eternity will be like for believers is beyond imagination, but each one can be thankful that God has such a perfect, beautiful plan for the future.

RESPOND

Read Romans 5:1-2 that reveals believers will one day share in God's glory. Share your appreciation of this with a fellow believer.

DAY 2

RECEIVE

Revelation 22:3-5

³ No longer will there be a curse upon anything. For the throne of God and of the Lamb will be there, and his servants will worship him. ⁴ And they will see his face, and his name will be written on their foreheads. ⁵ And there will be no night there—no need for lamps or sun—for the Lord God will shine on them. And they will reign forever and ever.

Genesis 3 tells of the curse that came on mankind and nature because of Adam's sin, but in eternity there will not be "a curse upon anything." The name of God will be written on the foreheads of believers, indicating ownership. There is darkness of nature and of sin now, but in eternity there will be no darkness for the God of light is there. Mention is made again of reigning with Him forever and ever.

REFLECT

Think of the contrast between now and then. Thank the Lord that all the trials now will be worth it when believers meet Him face to face.

RESPOND

Read 1 John 1:5-7 to be reminded that God is light and what this does for believers.

WEEK 39: REVELATION 22

RECEIVE

DAY 3

Revelation 22:6-7

⁶ Then the angel said to me, "Everything you have heard and seen is trustworthy and true. The Lord God, who inspires his prophets, has sent his angel to tell his servants what will happen soon." ⁷ "Look, I am coming soon! Blessed are those who obey the words of prophecy written in this book."

The apostle John had heard and seen many things, and now an angel assures him that all can be trusted and has been true. The same God who inspired the prophets to speak for Him and tell what would happen in the future has now sent His angel to tell what will happen soon. The Lord God is coming "soon." This word may have a time element of "without delay" and can also mean "quickly." Both are easy to see from God's perspective as He does not count time as we do and when He comes it will be quickly.

REFLECT

Revelation is telling about the end of time, but what is said about His coming is also true of the rapture of the Church when believers are caught up to meet Him in the air (see 1 Thessalonians 4:13-18). Are you ready when that time comes quickly?

RESPOND

Read 2 Peter 3:8-10 to see God does not reckon time as we do and why He is delaying His coming. Talk with a fellow believer about being ready to enter eternity with Jesus.

DAY 4

RECEIVE

Revelation 22:8-9

⁸ I, John, am the one who heard and saw all these things. And when I heard and saw them, I fell down to worship at the feet of the angel who showed them to me. ⁹ But he said, "No, don't worship me. I am a servant of God, just like you and your brothers the prophets, as well as all who obey what is written in this book. Worship only God!"

John was so overwhelmed with all he had seen and heard he wanted to worship the angel who had shown him everything. An angel is a created being, however, and he told John not to worship him but worship only God. This is also what Jesus told the devil when the devil wanted Him to worship him (see Matthew 4:10). Those who serve God are seen in this passage as angels, prophets, and those who obey what is written in Revelation. All are to worship "only God."

REFLECT

Does this further elevate God in your eyes to realize He is above the angels? No one should worship anything or anyone created, but only worship the Creator.

RESPOND

Notice how Hebrews 1:1-6 indicates Jesus is God by the heavenly Father's command for Him to be worshiped. Those who say Jesus is not God do not believe what God the Father has said.

WEEK 39: REVELATION 22

DAY 5

RECEIVE

Revelation 22:10-11

¹⁰ Then he instructed me, "Do not seal up the prophetic words in this book, for the time is near. ¹¹ Let the one who is doing harm continue to do harm; let the one who is vile continue to be vile; let the one who is righteous continue to live righteously; let the one who is holy continue to be holy."

John is commanded not to seal up the message of the book of Revelation. From the viewpoint of eternity, these events are near to occurring. From our perspective it is now much nearer than when John wrote these words. There is also a message about the destiny of people being determined by their decisions on earth. There is no chance to change one's eternal destiny after he or she passes from this earth (see Hebrews 9:27). The decision whether or not to trust in Jesus for salvation will have eternal consequences.

REFLECT

Does this impress on you the need to share your faith with others so they can believe in Jesus before it is too late? Once you have given the salvation message, live a life that honors Jesus before them. God may use you to draw others to Himself by drawing them through you.

RESPOND

Meet with a fellow Christ follower and pray for friends who need to trust in Jesus as Savior. Talk about how each of you can possibly be used so God can draw them to Himself through you.

WEEK 40: REVELATION 22

RECEIVE

DAY 1

Revelation 22:12-13

¹² "Look, I am coming soon, bringing my reward with me to repay all people according to their deeds. ¹³ I am the Alpha and the Omega, the First and the Last, the Beginning and the End."

The Lord Jesus speaks and says He is coming soon. Again, the word "soon" can mean "quickly." He will "repay all people according to their deeds." Jesus emphasized He is "the Beginning and the End" by saying He is "the Alpha and the Omega," the first and last letters of the Greek alphabet. This would include everything in between the beginning and the end.

REFLECT

Think of how great the Lord Jesus Christ is. He is everything you need. You can trust Him completely.

RESPOND

For other references to "Alpha and Omega," see Revelation 1:8 and 21:6 in addition to this one in Revelation 22:13. No doubt should be left about the greatness of the Lord Jesus Christ.

RECEIVE

DAY 2

Revelation 22:14-15

14 Blessed are those who wash their robes. They will be permitted to enter through the gates of the city and eat the fruit from the tree of life. 15 Outside the city are the dogs—the sorcerers, the sexually immoral, the murderers, the idol worshipers, and all who love to live a lie.

This passage reveals the blessedness of those inside the New Jerusalem and the destiny of those whose lives were characterized by the sins listed. "Sorcerers" is the word from which the word "pharmacy" or "drugs" is derived. "Idol worshipers" are those who worship what is created rather than the Creator. How wonderful it will be for those who are redeemed and how horrible it will be for those who are not.

REFLECT

Think how nothing else matches the riches of knowing Jesus as Savior. Pray for those who do not.

RESPOND

What can change the life of those enslaved by some of the sins mentioned in this passage? Read 1 Corinthians 6:9-11 to see that a relationship with Jesus can change such lives.

WEEK 40: REVELATION 22

DAY 3

RECEIVE

Revelation 22:16-17

[16] "I, Jesus, have sent my angel to give you this message for the churches. I am both the source of David and the heir to his throne. I am the bright morning star." [17] The Spirit and the bride say, "Come." Let anyone who hears this say, "Come." Let anyone who is thirsty come. Let anyone who desires drink freely from the water of life.

Jesus is the root and offspring of David. According to the flesh, Jesus came in the line of David and is the "heir to his throne." The bright morning star appears before sunrise. Jesus will catch up believers to meet Him in the air (see 1 Thessalonians 4:13-18). Later He will come to the earth in His second advent (see Revelation 19:11-16). Jesus offers salvation for anyone who will come to Him, but it must be done in this lifetime, not after death.

REFLECT

Be thankful for the person or ministry that brought you the message of salvation so you saw the need to trust in Jesus as Savior. Be a witness to tell others about Him.

RESPOND

With a Christian friend, talk about how each of you first heard the gospel and trusted in Jesus. Then talk about how you can take this gospel to others.

DAY 4

RECEIVE

Revelation 22:18-19

[18] And I solemnly declare to everyone who hears the words of prophecy written in this book: If anyone adds anything to what is written here, God will add to that person the plagues described in this book. [19] And if anyone removes any of the words from this book of prophecy, God will remove that person's share in the tree of life and in the holy city that are described in this book.

Some think this serious warning applies only to the book of Revelation. This book, however, quotes so much from the Old Testament and even the New Testament that one cannot change Revelation without changing the Bible. The 66 books in the Bible are the inspired canon of Scriptures. The Bible is the only book God has inspired, or breathed out to the human authors. No one is to add to or subtract from what the Bible teaches without suffering severe consequences.

REFLECT

Thank God that you have His revelation to make a lifetime of study. No one will ever know more about God than what is learned from the Scriptures.

RESPOND

Read Jude 1:3-4 to see that Jude considered God's revelation had been completed once for all and the urgency to share it with others.

WEEK 40: REVELATION 22

DAY 5

RECEIVE

Revelation 22:20-21

[20] He who is the faithful witness to all these things says, "Yes, I am coming soon!" Amen! Come, Lord Jesus! [21] May the grace of the Lord Jesus be with God's holy people.

This is a great closing to the book of Revelation. It is the promise of the coming of the Lord Jesus, and the affirmation of the apostle John for His coming. John had been persecuted for his faith. Others of the disciples had been martyred. Those who have been through such hardships would look forward to the Lord's return. The word "grace" is used frequently in the New Testament and is now used in closing the last book—"May the grace of the Lord Jesus be with God's holy people."

REFLECT

How is it with you? Have you had a hard life that causes you to look forward to the return of Jesus? If not, realize such times may come and the need to honor Him in your daily life now.

RESPOND

You have looked at 40 weeks of the study of Revelation with five posts in each week. Meet with a fellow Christ follower about what stands out to you as you think back over this study. Has it been impressed on you that in the end, Christ wins? There may be heartaches and grief in life, but final victory is assured. Knowing how the story ends can bring hope and assurance to believers. May the grace of God be with you.

Personal Notes

This is the tenth book I have been pleased to publish on Amazon.com with the help of others. Those I wish to especially express appreciation for are Richard Sanne, editorial assistant; Renee Fisher, self-publishing expert; and Nelly Murariu, graphic designer.

The following is a list of the ten books in the order they were published:

- *What They Believe: Studies of various religious groups*
- *Treasures from the Original, Vol. 1: 39 Greek Word Studies*
- *Treasures from the Original, Vol. 2: Studies in Philippians*
- *Treasures from the Original, Vol. 3: Studies in 2 Timothy*
- *John: An Eyewitness Report*
- *Genesis: Daily Scriptures to Receive, Reflect, and Respond*
- *Romans: Daily Scriptures to Receive, Reflect, and Respond*
- *Acts Volume 1: Daily Scriptures to Receive, Reflect, and Respond*
- *Acts Volume 2: Daily Scriptures to Receive, Reflect, and Respond*
- *Revelation: Daily Scriptures to Receive, Reflect, and Respond*

My prayer is that God will use these volumes to reveal to readers how to become right with God and to live to glorify Him.

Harold J. Berry
ThM, DD
Lincoln, Nebraska

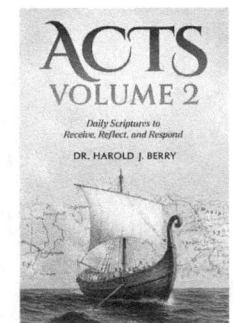

WWW.AMAZON.COM/STORES/AUTHOR/B07PH816C3

About the Author

Dr. Harold J. Berry is a former professor of Bible and Greek at Grace University of Omaha. He served for many years as personal assistant to Theodore H. Epp, founder of Back to the Bible. Dr. Berry holds a Master of Theology degree from Dallas Theological Seminary and a Doctor of Divinity from Grace University.

www.ingramcontent.com/pod-product-compliance
Lightning Source LLC
LaVergne TN
LVHW051400080426
835508LV00022B/2905